Emergency Vehicle Operations

A Line Officer's Guide

Second Edition

Emergency Vehicle Operations

A Line Officer's Guide

Second Edition

Raymond W. Beach, Jr.

Earl R. Morris

William C. Smith

CRC Press
Taylor & Francis Group
Boca Raton   London   New York

CRC Press is an imprint of the
Taylor & Francis Group, an informa business

Important Note

Products and services provided by K&M Publishers, Inc. are intended for educational purposes only. K&M Publishers, Inc. makes no warranties or guarantees, either expressed or implied, as to the legal effect of the information supplied in those products and services. Further, K&M Publishers, Inc. assumes no liability associated with providing this information. You are encouraged to seek the advice of your own legal counsel or that of your sponsoring agency or entity regarding this material.

ISBN 0-9727134-0-9

This book is dedicated with gratitude and respect to all the law enforcement officers who put their lives on the line every day.

.

In additions, the authors individually dedicate the books as follows:

To Joy, Bryan and Bobby, with love and respect.
—Raymond W. Beach, Jr.

To Darlene, Reena, Adam, Joni and Jordan for all of the patience, love and support.
—Earl R. Morris

To Ellen, Mackenzie and Cameron for the joy they bring to my life each and every day.
—William C. Smith

About the Authors

Raymond W. Beach, Jr. was the chairman of the national task force on emergency vehicle operations. This task force, organized by the International Association of Directors of Law Enforcement Standards and Training (IADLEST) and funded by the National Highway Traffic Safety Administration (NHTSA), produced the *Law Enforcement Driver Training Reference Guide 2000*. He is a nationally recognized expert and consultant on criminal justice matters and has written and lectured extensively on police policy and procedures as well as on the use of force. Mr. Beach is currently the Executive Director of the Michigan Commission on Law Enforcement Standards, a division of the Michigan Department of State Police.

Earl R. Morris was a member of the IADLEST/NHTSA task force and a twenty-three year veteran of law enforcement. He retired in July 2002 as the Colonel of the Utah Highway Patrol and as Deputy Commissioner for the Utah Department of Public Safety. He is a nationally recognized expert in the areas of emergency vehicle operations and the use of force, and he has published numerous articles on those subjects.

William C. Smith is an attorney and was the Legal Advisor for the IADLEST/NHTSA task force. He is also a Risk Management Consultant and was awarded the ARM designation from the Insurance Institute of America. Mr. Smith is the co-author of several books and numerous articles on the topic of police pursuit. He lives in Columbia, South Carolina.

Foreword

by

John T. Whetsel
Sheriff, Oklahoma County, Oklahoma and
Former President, International Association of Chiefs of Police

On June 23, 1980, a tragedy occurred. A mother and daughter were killed when their car was broadsided by a law enforcement vehicle involved in a high-speed pursuit. It was a scene that has been repeated far too often. However, from my perspective, this one was different. The innocent victims who died that day were my wife and youngest daughter.

At dusk, just after 9:00 p.m., an officer attempted to stop three motorcycles that were drag racing. Two quickly pulled over to the side of the road and gave up. The third kept going. The officer, who reportedly boasted about never losing a chase, decided to pursue the fleeing motorcycle for traffic violations.

The chase exceeded 100 miles per hour in a 45-m.p.h. zone. The motorcycle turned into a residential neighborhood with narrow streets and a 25-m.p.h. speed limit. Despite the location, neither the fleeing motorcycle nor the officer slowed down. In fact, the motorcycle began to pull away, building up a lead of nearly one half mile.

The pursuit crested a small hill and neared a busy intersection bordered by embankments overgrown with tall weeds. The motorcyclist ran the intersection stop sign without slowing. Seconds later, a small Nissan entered the intersection on the cross street. At that same moment, the officer roared over the hill, ran the stop sign and slammed into the side of the Nissan, impacting over 30 inches deep into the passenger compartment. Both vehicles traveled together for 68 feet. The patrol unit then went airborne for another 71 feet before hitting a utility pole. The Nissan skidded an additional 173 feet before striking an embankment and bursting into flames.

I was on my way home when I was dispatched to the accident scene to assist. I sat in the ambulance, reassuring the officer who was not seriously hurt. Then suddenly, in a horrible moment that will forever be etched in my mind, I realized that it was my wife's Nissan and that my family was involved. My oldest daughter, Stacy, was critically injured but survived. My wife, Darlene, age 27, and my youngest daughter, Rebecca, age 2, were not so lucky. They both died at the scene.

I am not saying that this particular incident is more tragic than any other simply because my family was involved. Any death as the result of law enforcement activities is a tragedy. However, you must understand the true cause of the incident.

While the fleeing suspect was clearly responsible, the officer must share the blame. Given all the factors involved, the pursuit should have been terminated. Instead, rather than acting in a professional manner, the officer made the pursuit a competition between the suspect and himself. This clouded his judgment, leading him to make the wrong decisions. Unfortunately, in this instance, they were deadly ones.

His agency has to share the blame as well. At the time of the incident, the officer had not been trained in emergency vehicle operations. So while the officer's decisions were his own, his agency did not help him make those decisions.

A decision to pursue is easy to make. It is much harder to know when not to pursue and when to terminate a pursuit. This book, written by experts, will help answer those questions. I strongly encourage you to take full advantage of this book, both by using it as a text in class and by keeping it as a reference guide afterwards.

Unfortunately, pursuits are necessary and will continue to occur. Some will end with the capture of armed robbers or rapists. Some will end with the issuance of traffic citations. Some will end without apprehensions. However, if you learn the material in this book and refer back to it often, you may never make the tragic discovery that I did. Some pursuits never end.

Contents

One

Why Should You Read This Book?

Objectives

After completing this chapter, you will be able to

- *Explain the importance of decision-making*
- *Use a "front end" approach for managing the risks of emergency vehicle operations*

$\mathbf{Y}$ou cannot learn to operate an emergency vehicle by reading a book. You learn by getting behind the wheel of your vehicle and actually operating it. So you may be wondering why you should take the time to read this book. The answer is simple. While the book does cover the basic aspects of vehicle operations, that is not the primary objective. What this book is really about is decision-making.

The Importance of Making the Right Decisions

Most tragic incidents involving emergency vehicles are not due to the lack of officer skills. They are the result of poor decisions on how to use those skills. Some questions you have to ask are

- When is an emergency really an emergency?
- Under what circumstances should you use emergency lights and siren?

1

- When should you pursue a fleeing suspect?
- When should a pursuit be called off?

Those are tough questions to answer. And if you make the wrong choice, your actions can lead to lawsuits and disciplinary actions. Even worse, the wrong choice can lead to serious injuries and fatalities. This book can help you make the right decisions and manage the risks that you face.

When it comes to managing the risks of emergency vehicle operations, you have to take a "front end" approach. By front end, we mean that **you have to anticipate what your risks will be and know how to handle them before they occur**. When you are confronted with an emergency situation, you will not have time to refer back to this book or to your agency's policy. All you can do is evaluate the situation as best you can and make a decision. A "front end" approach helps ensure that those decisions are safe and in line with agency policy.

To anticipate what your risks will be, you have to know what to expect. This book explains how the various modes of emergency vehicle operations differ from one another and gives some ideas on how to approach the situations that you will face. The book even goes so far as to tell you how those situations will affect you, both mentally and physically. Then by using your agency's policy as a guideline, you can refine these ideas into a system for handling all aspects of vehicle operations. Through constant practice, that system will become second nature, leading to better decision-making.

You Are the Key to Training

The key to successful training is you. You have to combine the information in this book with a complete understanding of your agency's policy on emergency vehicle operations. You then have to take that knowledge out of the classroom and onto the street, where it must be merged with safe operator techniques.

2

It is a lot of work, but the rewards of that work are clear. By making an effort at the front end, you stand a good chance of not becoming another tragic statistic.

Review Questions

1. What is the most common cause of tragic incidents involving emergency vehicles?

2. What is meant by "front end" risk management? How can you benefit from it?

Legal and Risk
Management Aspects

Two

What Is Liability?

Objectives

After completing this chapter, you will be able to

- *Understand the types of liability*
- *Identify the types of damages you would have to pay if found to be liable for an injury*

Over the past several years, emergency vehicle operations have been among the most highly litigated areas of law enforcement. Before getting behind the wheel of a patrol car, you need to understand the legal risks you are taking. When you know your risks, you can take steps to protect yourself.

Background on Lawsuits

Lawsuits may arise under state or federal law. In state law proceedings, a lawsuit arising from law enforcement activities revolves around a **tort**. For our purposes, the term "tort" will refer to a claim under state law. (Federal law claims, which we discuss later in this book, arise from the violation of a constitutional protection and are sometimes referred to as "constitutional" torts. Those claims are very different from tort claims under state law.)

A tort is a private or civil wrong against a person for which a court may award money to the injured person. The person who was injured and initiates the lawsuit is known as the

plaintiff. The **defendant** is the person or entity accused of causing the injury. If you are the defendant, the plaintiff tries to prove that you were responsible for the injury. Being held legally responsible for the plaintiff's injuries is referred to as being "liable" for the injuries. Liability is a state of legal responsibility for some wrong that you have caused. If you are held liable, then the plaintiff is entitled to compensation from you. This is known as **paying damages**.

Just as the types of injury vary, so do the types of liability. For emergency vehicle operations, there are two types of state tort liability:

- Direct liability
- Vicarious liability

One or both may apply for any given case. The distinction between them is important because the type of liability claim may determine things such as which court hears the case, who is the defendant(s), and what sort of compensation is available to the plaintiff.

Direct Liability

As the name implies, **direct liability** is based upon a direct cause of injury to the plaintiff. More simply stated, it's your action (or inaction) that directly resulted in the plaintiff's injury. Claims of direct liability generally fall into one of two types:

- Negligence
- Willful misconduct

Negligence, sometimes called **simple negligence**, does not involve an intentional act on your part. Instead it is an unintentional failure to exercise a reasonable degree of care. Unfortunately, there is not a uniform standard on what is reasonable. Although courts use a standard of care known as "the reasonable man" standard to evaluate the reasonableness of your behavior in a set of circumstances, there seem to be as many definitions of reasonableness as there are court cases. However, by having written policies and procedures, your agency has determined what it considers to be reasonable. As long as you follow your agency's guidelines, you generally will be protected from claims of simple negligence based upon your work-related conduct.

An officer's acts of simple negligence are generally excluded from tort liability by virtue of protections found in a state's **tort claims statutes**. Tort claims statutes are generally designed to give an injured party a limited right to sue public employees, such as the police. However, these statutes usually limit the amount that a plaintiff can recover as damages, and they often prevent certain persons, such as individual officers, from being sued personally. Tort claims statutes differ from state to state, so you should consult your department's legal advisor to learn what protection your state statutes provide you.

In addition to simple negligence, there are more aggravated levels of negligence. **Gross negligence** is unreasonable conduct to such an extent that you should have known an injury was likely to happen. Beyond gross negligence is **reckless behavior**, sometimes referred to as **reckless negligence** or **willful and wanton negligence**. This involves conduct that basically displays extreme indifference to the consequences of one's own actions.

The line between the various levels of negligence can be hard to draw. For instance, driving fifty miles an hour in a thirty miles-per-hour zone might be considered negligent, especially if you are in a non-emergency mode. In bad weather, however, the same behavior may be classified as grossly negligent or even reckless. Other factors will impact the degree of negligence, too. They include the time of day, presence of pedestrians and the volume of traffic. An officer's gross negligence, reckless behavior or other aggravated negligence may not be protected under a state's tort claims act, with the result being that the officer may be held personally responsible for injuries caused to the plaintiff.

No matter what level of negligence, they all have one thing in common: the injury or damage was unintentional. This is important because "intent" is a key to the type of damages that a court can award. In a negligence case, the plaintiff can only be awarded **compensatory damages**, sometimes known as **actual** or **special damages**. This is money that compensates for the injury only. Since the actions causing the injury were unintentional, no additional money will be awarded to the plaintiff as a punishment to the wrongdoer. The extent of the injury sets the amount of the compensation. Again, it is important to keep in mind that where the plaintiff alleges your simple negligence was a cause of injury, your state Tort Claims Act will likely provide you protection from personal liability.

In every situation where a plaintiff claims that you were negligent, there must be a fact-specific evaluation of the reasonableness of your conduct. This evaluation must be based upon the circumstances that gave rise to the plaintiff's injury. In other words, the reasonableness of your conduct will be based on the particulars of your specific case.

Separate from an act of negligence is one that involves an **intentional tort**. An intentional tort differs from negligence in that it involves a conscious decision to engage in the injury-causing behavior or an intentional disregard of the safety of others. In other words, you knew that your behavior was wrong, but you did it anyway.

In a situation involving an intentional tort, you may be forced to pay compensatory damages if you caused the injury. But since you made a conscious decision to act as you did, it is possible that you might also be "punished" for your behavior. Normally the punishment is the awarding of additional money to a plaintiff over and above the compensatory levels. The additional money is known as **punitive damages**. The purpose of a court's awarding punitive damages goes beyond compensating the plaintiff. It also serves as a deterrent to keep you from engaging in such behavior again in the future.

It is also possible that an act of willful or intentional misconduct might result in criminal prosecution. This is what happens when an officer's behavior is so far removed from any standard of reasonableness that a court may conclude that the officer possessed an intent to specifically harm an individual that rises to the level of criminal behavior. A classic example of this type behavior is when officers beat a submissive, non-resisting defendant at the end of a vehicular pursuit to vent their frustration. Such behavior could lead to criminal charges of assault and battery in state court and charges of criminal violation of civil rights in federal court.

You must understand that a law enforcement agency's liability insurance coverage for its officers does not typically cover intentional or criminal acts committed by its officers. Also, officers who commit intentional or criminal acts generally are stripped of any protection afforded them by state tort claim statutes. This means that officers who engage in willful misconduct may be subject to both criminal prosecution and civil suits in which they personally may be responsible for any award of damages. In other words, the money for any damages may come out of your own pocket.

Sometimes acts of intentional misconduct rise to the level of **constitutional torts**. This is a highly important concept where a plaintiff brings suit under the federal civil rights statute known as **Title 42, United States Code Section 1983**, which will be discussed in more detail in the next chapter. Unlike negligence suits, suits brought under Section 1983 are not subject to any limitation on damages. Likewise, your state Tort Claims Act will not provide you any protection from liability in the Section 1983 action. These suits are more likely to result in damages being awarded against the individual officer.

Vicarious Liability

You are not the only one who may be liable for your actions. It is possible that your supervisors and other senior officials may be subject to liability proceedings, as well. Whenever someone is held responsible for the actions of another, this is known as **indirect** or **vicarious liability**.

The word "vicarious" means "acting in the place of someone else." Vicarious liability can be claimed when a plaintiff has suffered an injury at the hands of an officer who was improperly supervised, trained or otherwise allowed to cause the injury by the action or inaction of a senior official. In other words, if you are not supervised or trained properly, then those responsible for your supervision and training may be held responsible for your actions that cause injury to others.

Some people refer to vicarious liability as being the same as a theory of imputed negligence liability called **respondeat superior**, which is Latin for "let the master answer." However, this is not legally correct. Respondeat superior liability cannot be imposed against a superior or supervising officer. It can be imposed only against the agency. The theory is that your employing agency should be liable for your negligence simply because you work for it. For that to happen, though, the actions perceived to be negligent must be within the course and scope of your employment when the plaintiff's injury occurred. The claim is that the injury would not have occurred if you were not carrying out your duties as a law enforcement officer. Since you were acting in an official capacity, your agency should be responsible. Respondeat superior liability is a theory of imputed negligence and is a type of direct liability.

On the other hand, vicarious liability may occur when a supervisor takes (or does not take) action that contributes to the injury. In emergency vehicle operations, cases of vicarious liability usually arise when field supervisors fail to exercise proper control over a pursuit as required by the agency's policy or by statute. As an example, say a supervisor allows you to ram the vehicle of a fleeing suspect when the department has a "no ramming" policy. If the suspect or an innocent third party is injured, the supervisor may be held liable for permitting the improper procedure.

Typically, vicarious liability falls into a category of negligence. As such, plaintiffs are entitled only to compensatory damages from senior officials. However, if a supervisor acted intentionally, then that is not a case of vicarious liability; it is **direct liability**. To prove the direct liability of a supervisor, a plaintiff must show that the senior official knew there was a high probability of an injury but directed the subordinate to act anyway, or ratified the subordinate's conduct, which the supervisor knew was clearly not permissible or lawful.

Civil Rights Violations (42 USC Section 1983)

Virtually every emergency vehicle civil rights claim will be brought under a federal statute known as Section 1983. Section 1983 is found in Title 42 of the United States Code. It allows an injured person to bring a civil lawsuit for damages if the injury resulted from a violation of a federal constitutional right or other federal law, and if the injury was caused by a person acting "under color of state law."

Violations of Section 1983 always involve intentional or deliberate acts, which is one way in which Section 1983 claims differ from state tort claims. In the state tort actions, a plaintiff almost always claims that his/her injury was caused by an officer's negligent actions, although sometimes the plaintiff will allege intentional tort as well. In a civil rights case, however, the injury is claimed to have resulted from an officer's intentional violation of a constitutional right belonging to the injured party. The amount of damages the plaintiff can recover is not limited in Section 1983 claims, as it may be under a state's tort claims act, as it might be the case under a state's Tort Claims Act.

Section 1983 actions, while based upon a federal statute, can be brought in either state or federal court. Liability under Section 1983 may be direct or indirect, just as it may be for state torts. The liability of an employer, or municipal liability, however, is very different under Section 1983.

Municipal Liability under Section 1983

From the standpoint of financial recovery, **municipal liability** is the most devastating type of liability. It is the one people hear about on television and read about in the newspapers. Recovery comes from the "deep pockets" of the municipal treasury and is often in the millions of dollars.

A municipality, defined as any entity of government below the state level, cannot be held liable under Section 1983 simply because it employs an officer who caused an injury. There must be some fault on the part of the local government. To prove this, a plaintiff must show that a policy of the municipality was the moving force behind the injury caused by the officer. It is important to understand that the policy does not have to be a written one; it can simply be the custom or practice of the local law enforcement agency. Although a single act by an officer who is not a policy maker cannot establish a policy, repeated incidents of unlawful practices by line officers can be viewed as creating the custom or practice of the department. These practices could become the agency's "policy" and thereby expose the agency and its municipality to liability.

An example of a flawed policy is one that requires nothing more than officers "exercising good judgment" when it comes to vehicle operations. The problem is that the policy is too vague; it provides no real guidelines. If an officer violates the constitutional rights of a suspect or an innocent third party whose rights were clearly established at the time of the injury, there is a good chance that the municipality will be held liable.

A municipality must do more than just have good policies. It must also provide adequate training on implementing them. Recent court decisions have stated that a failure to train may show **deliberate indifference** to the rights of the citizens of the community. The theory is that if a city puts inadequately trained officers on the street, someone is going to get hurt needlessly. Deliberate indifference is considered a case of extreme disregard for public safety and opens the door to municipal liability.

Review Questions

1. What is a tort?

2. Who are the two parties in a civil case?

3. What are the various types of liability? Explain the difference between them.

4. Which type of liability usually results in the highest level of monetary damages? Why is that?

5. What are the two categories of direct liability? How are they different from each other?

6. What is the difference between compensatory damages and punitive damages? Under what circumstances are each awarded?

7. When can a claim of vicarious liability be made?

8. What is meant when a municipality is accused of "deliberate indifference?"

Three

The Basis of Lawsuits

Objectives

After completing this chapter, you will be able to

- *Explain what duties are and how they are created*
- *State the requirements needed for your vehicle to be exempt from traffic laws during emergency responses and pursuits*
- *Understand when you may have "good faith" immunity from acts of negligence*

In the previous chapter, we discussed the various types of liability that can affect emergency vehicle operations. Now we move on to how liability is established. Understanding how a lawsuit comes about will help you take proactive steps to avoid one.

What Is a Duty?

The mere fact that an officer was involved in some sort of accident is not sufficient reason to impose liability on the agency or officer. People who are injured must establish that law enforcement personnel were legally responsible for the injury. To do that, plaintiffs have to show that there was an obligation, or **duty**, to protect them. A duty may not obligate an agency and its officers to protect all citizens at all times, but it does obligate them not to injure somebody. If you are sued, the plaintiff will try to prove that he or she was injured because you neglected a duty. Typically, duties regarding emergency vehicle operations arise three ways:

- By state statute or law
- By agency policy
- By constitutional provision

Duties Created by State Statute or Law

Most states do not have statutory provisions that specifically govern the non-emergency operation of an emergency vehicle. Instead, **non-emergency operations usually falls under the same laws that regulate the general motoring public.** If you are in a non-emergency mode, you must obey the same rules and regulations as everyone else. Any violation of a traffic law may be considered an act of negligence. If you are involved in a collision while performing an illegal maneuver, such as speeding or making an illegal U-turn, you may be held responsible for any injury or damage. In some states, the violation of a statute in and of itself and without any discussion of the circumstances surrounding the violation is regarded as negligence. This is known as **negligence per se**.

On the other hand, every state has an emergency vehicle statute to govern emergency response and pursuit situations. This statute is designed to give you the authority to do your job while at the same time taking into account the safety of the general public. The exact wording of the statutes varies from state to state, but they do have similarities. In most areas, **the driver of an emergency vehicle is authorized to disregard many traffic laws when responding to emergencies**. To be exempt from these laws, however, you must take certain steps.

Steps Required to Be Exempt from Traffic Laws

- **Use audible and visual signals.** Most states require that both warning lights and sirens (or some other audible warning device) be used in all emergency and pursuit situations, unless there is a specific reason not to use them. In other states, you only need to use one of your emergency signals to qualify for a traffic law exemption. Some states statutes may allow exceptions to using lights and sirens when officers are engaged in activities such as conducting certain types of surveillance or responding to an alarm call where use of the lights and siren might not be desirable. Any exemptions such as these allowed by your state will be specifically set out in the state statute.

• **Drive with due regard for public safety.** In legal terms, due regard is the absence of negligence. In relation to emergency vehicle operations, this means that you recognize operating in an emergency mode can be dangerous to the general public. To act with due regard for public safety, you must keep an eye toward protecting not just innocent third parties, but everyone who could conceivably be affected by the emergency response or pursuit. In a pursuit, this includes both you and the suspect you are pursuing.

State statutes and regulations can have other implications for the driver of an emergency vehicle as well. In some states, provisions set forth in either statute or regulation require specialized driver training for officers. There may be a requirement that officers be trained for emergency or pursuit responses before taking part in one. The provisions may go further by mandating that all officers be certified in these areas as opposed to just receiving training. Officers in some states may even have their law enforcement certifications revoked if they engage in reckless behaviors involving use of emergency vehicles. In addition, state statutes and regulations may require that all agencies create policies to govern emergency vehicle activities and that they train to the policies.

Duties Created by Policy

Simply defined, a policy is a directive for action. The policies of a law enforcement agency are guidelines for the actions and behaviors of its officers. By establishing what an officer's responsibilities are, these guidelines are the duties created by policy. In many cases, agencies take the broad duties created by the state statutes and tailor them to fit the needs of their individual communities. An agency's policy serves both as a means of exerting control over officer actions and a means of identifying permissible discretion for its officers. Control and discretion are important components of the agency's Emergency Vehicle Operations Risk Management Program. The concept of a departmental risk management program is discussed in the next chapter.

As a law enforcement officer, **you must know and completely understand your agency's policy on emergency vehicle operations**. A breach of a duty created by your agency could lead to direct liability on your part. If a plaintiff claims you caused an injury by failing to carry out your agency's policy, you may be held liable due to your negligence or intentional misconduct.

In addition, you cannot exceed the scope of what the policy allows. If you do, you could find yourself confronted with another liability problem. For instance, your agency may consider ramming an acceptable use of deadly force to stop an extremely dangerous suspect. If you use that maneuver, it must be applied in a way that is considered reasonable. Should a court decide that your use of the force was so excessive that it was unreasonable, you could be held liable for any injury, even though your agency sanctions ramming.

Keep in mind that the use of deadly force applied with a vehicle has the same purpose as deadly force applied with a firearm: to stop a threat. You can never use deadly force as a means to punish a suspect. Deadly force must always be used in compliance with the constitutional limitations imposed upon its usage by the United States Supreme Court.

Duties Created by Constitutional Provision

The last way a duty can be established is by a constitutional provision. This can be through the U.S. Constitution or that of your individual state. In emergency vehicle operations, two U.S. constitutional amendments are particularly important.

The first of these is the **Fourth Amendment**. It usually comes into play when **a suspect suffers an injury** at the hand of a pursuing officer. The Fourth Amendment protects all citizens from unreasonable searches and seizures. It is possible that a suspect having been injured could be judged an unreasonable seizure if the injury was the result of something the officer did intentionally.

One of the best known cases on pursuit-related seizures is *Brower v. Inyo County*. In the *Brower* case, some sheriff's deputies decided to stop a suspect fleeing them in a stolen car by setting up a roadblock. The roadblock consisted of pulling an eighteen-wheel tractor trailer across both lanes of a two-lane highway, a short distance beyond a blind curve. Additionally, the spotlight of a cruiser was trained at eye-level and aimed at the apex of the curve. When the suspect came around the curve, he was blinded by the spotlight and crashed into the tractor-trailer. The suspect died in the collision. The U.S. Supreme Court did not decide whether that particular seizure was unreasonable, but it did state the roadblock was a seizure by use of deadly force.

Roadblocks are not the only activities that may be considered "seizures." Any intentional contact is likely to raise a Fourth Amendment claim. The message to officers and policy makers is that the reasonableness of any contact activity should be worked out in advance. The decision on "what is allowed" and "how each contact should be applied" needs to be accurately communicated to all personnel in the department by policy and training. The training should be sufficiently thorough that all officers are able to apply the policy without hesitation.

This is especially true in cases involving the department's authorization to use the Pursuit Immobilization Technique (PIT), sometimes referred to as Tactical Vehicle Intervention (TVI). PIT/TVI is a maneuver where an officer intentionally uses his or her emergency vehicle to push a suspect vehicle at an angle from the rear, causing the suspect vehicle to spin out of control so that apprehension can be effected. Before an officer can be authorized to use this maneuver, that officer must be aware in great detail of the circumstances under which the maneuver can be successfully applied and the impact of the vehicle dynamics involved.

Tactics such as PIT/TVI require extensive training before they can be used and also require specific policy guidance. It is also critical that an agency coordinates its Use of Force continuum to address vehicle tactics that may be considered "seizures" such as the ramming or PIT/TVI of a vehicle.

It is important to understand that the Fourth Amendment does not restrict you from seizing a suspect. Only "unreasonable" seizures are prohibited. As long as your department has a clear and comprehensive policy regarding pursuits and trains you to implement it, you probably will not have a problem.

The second constitutional amendment that may create a duty "not to injure" is the **Fourteenth Amendment**. Most claims based on this amendment arise from **an injury to an innocent third party**. The critical aspect of the Fourteenth Amendment states that no citizen can be denied the right of life, liberty or property without due process of law. When bystanders are injured, they will often claim they were denied that right.

Since 1998, however, the use of the Fourteenth Amendment as a basis for liability against law enforcement officers has diminished somewhat. In *County of Sacramento v. Lewis*, the U.S. Supreme Court determined that an officer's conduct must "shock the conscience" of the court before a third-party plaintiff could successfully establish a Section 1983 claim against the officer for injuries sustained in a vehicular pursuit. The "shocks the conscience" standard is a significantly higher standard than either the "reckless conduct" or "deliberate indifference" standards which previously had been viewed as appropriate for such conduct by some federal appeals courts.

In the *Lewis* case, a deputy chased a suspect driving a motorcycle at high speed. When the suspect lost control, the suspect's passenger was thrown from the motorcycle and was then hit by the pursuing deputy's vehicle. The passenger was killed. The issue in the *Lewis* case was whether a law enforcement officer could be seen to violate the Fourteenth Amendment's guarantee of substantive due process by causing somebody's death through a deliberate or reckless indifference to life in a high-speed pursuit. The Supreme Court decision stated that, given the circumstances, only an intention by the officer to cause harm unrelated to the legitimate apprehension of the suspect could lead the Court to view the officer's conduct as being "shocking to the conscience."

It is important to remember, however, that the facts in the *Lewis* case are very limited and do not mean a Fourteenth Amendment claim will not be sustained under appropriate circumstances. The Court's ruling might have been very different if the officer had used deadly force to ram the fleeing motorcycle, thereby crushing the passenger in the process of making a "seizure." It is also important to remember that the *Lewis* case does not affect the right of an injured third party to bring a state tort action against a pursuing officer. Just because a Section 1983 case may not stand up does not mean that a state tort claim will fail as well.

Another point to keep in mind about third party injury claims is that both the fleeing suspect and you could be sued if the injury occurred as the result of a pursuit. However, the focus of attention is rarely on the person being chased. First, suspects do not have the "deep pockets" potential that a municipality has. Second, they do not have a constitutional duty to protect the public.

Instead, most plaintiffs concentrate on the officer involved in the incident. If this happens to you, expert witnesses will be called to testify whether your conduct met with generally accepted law enforcement standards. If your behavior is ruled to have violated the constitutional rights of the injured party, some effort will probably be made to show that your behavior was due to inadequate training or a defective policy. In this manner, a plaintiff attempts to attach municipal liability. Should that happen, you may be off the hook, but your agency and municipality might be required to pay a huge amount of money in damages. From your standpoint, your best guarantee of protection is discussed next.

Protecting Yourself in the Event of a Lawsuit

All of this legal information can be confusing. But you do not need to go to law school to know how to protect yourself against liability in the event of a lawsuit. And you do not have to consult with an attorney before handling any assigned task. All you have to do is **comply with your agency's policy at all times**.

Your agency's policy will protect you from most claims of liability. Under the legal concept of **qualified immunity**, also known as **"good faith" immunity**, you may not be held liable for behavior that does not violate "clearly established law." In other words, your agency's policy provides the guidelines under which you operate. As long as you stay within those guidelines, you will most likely be protected.

Unlike you, however, a law enforcement agency is not entitled to "good faith" immunity. Failure to have a meaningful policy may subject a department to liability, even where administrators have provided some guidance. It is up to your agency to outline a clear and comprehensive policy that can withstand a challenge in court and to provide proper training to implement it. Of course, once you have been trained on the policy, you are obligated to follow it.

Review Questions

1. What is a duty? How does it relate to a liability claim?

2. What are your state's statutory provisions regarding non-emergency and emergency vehicle operations?

3. In your state, are there circumstances where you are allowed to engage in emergency response driving without using your emergency lights or siren? If so, what are those circumstances?

4. What does "due regard for public safety" mean?

5. What is a policy?

6. How does the Fourth Amendment to the U.S. Constitution affect law enforcement driving?

7. How does the Fourteenth Amendment affect law enforcement driving?

8. What is the best way to protect yourself against lawsuits?

Four

Risk Management for Emergency Vehicle Operations

Objectives

After completing this chapter, you will be able to

- *State the four basic steps of an effective risk management process*
- *Explain the difference between behind-the-wheel risk management and departmental risk management*
- *Identify two benefits of a successful risk management program*

In the previous two chapters, we discussed the various types of liability and the basis for lawsuits brought against law enforcement officers. Now we move on to a discussion of risk management. An effective risk management program can help limit liability and increase your confidence and the department's confidence that your emergency vehicle operations are providing a valuable community service.

Basic Risk Management

Risk management is a fairly simple idea. The objective is to identify things that may cause injury or harm and then take steps to prevent them from happening. People speak of risk in terms of exposure, such as taking a certain action exposes you to a possible hazard. Each time you respond to an emergency call or pursue an offender, there are numerous risks, or potential hazards, which you must face. These risks are called the **"Universe of Risks"** and can be divided into two categories:

- **Known Risks**—Risks that an officer should be aware of and can anticipate. From an emergency vehicle operations standpoint, known risk might include:
  —Your physical condition
  —The condition of your vehicle
  —The type of call you are responding to
  —The environment of the response

- **Unknown Risks**—Risks that are unpredictable. These are the risks that you have no control over. They might include:
  —The reactions of pedestrians and drivers of other vehicles to your warning devices
  —The driving behavior of the suspect you are pursuing
  —The response behaviors of assisting officers

Risk management in emergency vehicle operations is about predicting the risk factors involved in either emergency response or pursuit activities and being prepared to either avoid those risks or respond appropriately to them. This is done using a four-step method.

Steps for Effective Risk Management

1. Identify and analyze all known risks.
2. Determine ways to reduce the impact of these risks.
3. Implement the best possible solution.
4. Monitor the solution for effectiveness and adjust as necessary.

These four steps should be performed both by the department and by the officers on the street.

Department Risk Management

There are many benefits of effective departmental risk management. The greatest is that officers develop a higher confidence in their capabilities and in the department's ability to support them. An offshoot of that is the public develops a greater confidence in its law enforcement agency. Other benefits include decreased losses due to injuries and property damage, lower insurance premiums, and an increase in the department's ability to defend itself and its officers in the event of a lawsuit.

Effective departmental risk management programs cover three crucial elements:

1. Policy development
2. Comprehensive training
3. Incident review

Policy development is the crucial first step. The policy represents a guide for decision-making that protects both the officer and the public during a response. A policy puts restraints on you by detailing what you cannot do as well as identifying areas where you have discretion on what actions you can take. Basically, a policy should attempt to address the known risks of emergency vehicle operations.

Critical Questions that a Policy Should Address

- For what offense you can initiate a pursuit?
- What are your alternatives to pursuing a suspect?
- What circumstances require you terminate a pursuit even if you have not apprehended the suspect?
- What types of force can you use to end a pursuit and when can you use them?
- What are the minimum communication and technology requirements for emergency responses and pursuits?

We need to make three final points about policy. First, the success of any policy depends on the "buy in" of the department's executive leadership as well as the line staff. A statement by the head of an agency that the department will manage EVO risks is useless if a "run 'em 'til the wheels fall off" atmosphere prevails. There must be recognition from the top down that the department's EVO policies which have been developed to identify permissible officer actions will be enforced, with administrative discipline if necessary.

Second, a policy cannot be successful if it is not based on "the real world." If line officers view a policy as being unworkable, it has little chance of successful implementation on the street.

Finally, every EVO policy should state that only officers who complete comprehensive EVO training may participate in pursuit activities. A policy should address the known risks of emergency vehicle operations, and it must also include a provision for training in behind-the-wheel decision-making in order to account for the unknown risks. This provision is so crucial that it should be included in an EVO policy, even if state law or regulation does not mandate such training.

As just stated, an officer who has not been trained must never engage in a pursuit. This is why **comprehensive training** is crucial. Every emergency response and pursuit will be different. While a policy can account for the known risks, you have to make behind-the-wheel decisions about the unknown risks, which will vary with each incident. You must be able to evaluate unfolding risks and decide on appropriate courses of action. This is of equal or greater importance than the technical ability to control your vehicle in a variety of environments. This skill can be developed through training.

Factors on which to Base EVO Training

- **Officer awareness of response options**—An awareness of response options comes about through familiarity with both permissible options under the department's policy and an understanding of how to apply those options. For example, if your department which permits the use of the Pursuit Immobilization Technique (PIT) or Tactical Vehicle Intervention (TVI) maneuver, you must understand not only how to perform the maneuver but also when the maneuver may be effective. A decision to attempt a PIT/TVI during rush hour traffic in a congested area could have drastic results. Therefore, it may not be a response option under certain circumstances, even though your policy permits its use for the offense the officer is pursuing. On the other hand, if your policy does not sanction PIT/TVI, then there is no room for discretion. The PIT/TVI maneuver must never be used.

- **Controlled response selection and implementation**—Policy will detail your options, but you still need to decide which option to use and then implement it properly. Your ability to make these decisions may be clouded by the adrenaline surge that accompanies an emergency response or pursuit. It is crucial that you control that surge so you can make the best decisions. Training can help you do this, just as similar training helps professional pilots communicate clearly and calmly about the situations they confront while in the air.

The final piece of department risk management is **incident review**. Using past experience in a positive way can be the best means of preparing officers for the future and protecting the public and the department. An agency should require officers to complete after-action reports after each incident, even if no physical injury or property damage occurred. These reports should be analyzed, documented and incorporated into policy development and training. Agencies that do not learn from past mistakes may be destined to repeat them.

Departments should not limit their analysis to just their own experiences. They can learn from the experiences of other law enforcement agencies as well. All incidents, even those that do not result in lawsuits and those that occurred in other jurisdictions, are valuable learning opportunities. Exposure to the "worst case" in training frequently keeps the worst case from becoming a reality.

Line Officer Risk Management

As stated earlier, you face numerous risks each time you respond to an emergency call or engage in a pursuit. Effective management of these risks begins with what is known as the **interactive triangle**.

The interactive triangle is the interplay of three components in any response or pursuit: the driver, the vehicle, and the environment where the incident takes place. You are able to control only one of these components. At the time of a pursuit, you cannot control the condition of your vehicle. It is how it is, although it must be in good working order for you to contemplate a pursuit. The same is true for the environment. You cannot control where the incident occurs or under what conditions. The only aspect you can control is you, the driver. That is where you should direct your risk management efforts.

Risk management by a line officer is primarily an exercise in effective decision-making. That is crucial to accomplishing your law enforcement mission and protecting the public from unreasonable risks. These decisions are just as important as your physical and technical abilities to control your vehicle. The foundations for making the best decisions are directly related to the department's risk management activities.

Foundations of Line Officer Risk Management

- **Know your agency's policy**—An effective agency policy addresses the known risks of an emergency response or pursuit, and details what you can and cannot do in an incident. You cannot make a good decision if you do not know your options. You must also constantly keep in mind that you are obligated to follow your policy and to behave objectively and reasonably, regardless of your personal feelings.

- **Participate in training**—Training enhances your skills in controlling your vehicle in various situations and increases your ability to make good decisions behind the wheel. Your agency must provide you training, but it is up to you to apply the principles learned in training.

- **Participate in incident reviews**—Incident reviews are not meant to be forms of disciplinary actions. By analyzing what went wrong and what went right, you have an opportunity to learn from your experiences and increase your confidence for the next incident. Also, incident reviews allow you to provide feedback on the effectiveness of the agency's policy. Since you must abide by your policy, it is crucial that the policy reflects the "real world" situations you face on the street.

Periodically, line officers and management need to review their risk management efforts in light of changing laws and enforcement strategies. The last step of the basic four-step process, the **feedback component**, is what makes the process a proactive one. Only by frequently updating their programs can agencies and line officers continue to manage the risks they face and maintain high-levels of service for the communities they protect.

Review Questions

1. The "Universe of Risks" can be divided into two categories. What are they?

2. What are the four steps of a comprehensive risk management program?

3. What are the three elements of risk management at the department level?

4. What is the definition of risk?

5. Which component of the interactive triangle is not a risk factor?

6. Identify two examples of unknown risks.

7. Explain how the terms "control" and "discretion" apply to an EVO policy.

Non-Emergency Operations

Five

The Foundation of Emergency Vehicle Operations

Objectives

After completing this chapter, you will be able to

- *Identify the unique characteristics of emergency vehicle operations*
- *Identify the components of safe driving*
- *Utilize a driving system to increase your efficiency and safety*
- *Understand the role that occupant protection devices play in officer survival*

Most officers begin an emergency vehicle training course with a number of set driving habits. Some of these habits are good; others are not. Even if your driving record is spotless, you probably have a few areas that could use improvement. This chapter lays the foundation for doing that.

Unique Characteristics of Emergency Vehicle Operations

In order to be a safe driver, you must understand the unique characteristics of emergency vehicle operations. This helps you eliminate incorrect perceptions of your job and increases your chances of demonstrating correct knowledge, skills and behaviors.

Characteristics of Emergency Vehicle Operations

- You must comply with state laws and agency policy at all times.
- The general public will react to the sight of a law enforcement vehicle.
- You must maintain your community's expectations. These include complying with all motor vehicle laws, acting as a positive example, and being ready to respond to a sudden emergency.
- Use and monitor a radio and other equipment such as car phones and computers while driving.
- Frequently drive while under emotional stress.
- Deal with distractions caused by transporting individuals under arrest, DWI suspects and others.
- Observe buildings, vehicles and people while driving.

The Components of Driving

When the act of driving is analyzed, there are really only three components. First is **awareness**. This is the recognition of changes in the traffic environment which could disrupt your vehicle's movement. Second is **space management**, which is planning ahead to keep the best control of your path of travel. Last is **collision avoidance**, accomplished by moving your vehicle into an alternate path of travel whenever necessary.

To effectively perform all three components, you must enhance your perception skills. These are the skills that enable you to recognize what is happening around you and to predict what may happen based upon what you see. There are two steps that you can take to minimize distractions and focus on the most critical details.

Rules for Improving Your Perceptual Skills

- **Distribute your attention over large areas.** Do not concentrate on any area for more than two seconds at a time. Keeping your eyes moving reduces the chance that you will miss something important.

- **Search ahead of the vehicle.** This gives you a chance to spot and react to traffic scenes that are deteriorating. A good rule is to search ahead ten to twelve seconds. This means you should evaluate the distance your vehicle will travel at your current speed in ten to twelve seconds.

Driving Systems

One way to maximize your perception skills is to employ a proven driving system. A driving system is a series of steps designed to maximize the low-risk, high-gain operation of a vehicle. There are a number of good systems. Three of the most common are detailed below. Your agency may advocate one of them or possibly a different one. Whichever system your agency chooses is the one you must master.

The **Smith System** was the first driving system to recognize the need to learn perceptual as well as manipulative skills. It features five steps.

- **"Aim High in Driving."** Keep your view "up" rather than just "down" at the area in front of you. At a minimum, maintain an active view of one block ahead in city traffic.

- **"Keep Your Eyes Moving."** Continually look around you. Check near and far every few seconds. Also check to the left and right, in the mirrors and at the instrument panel.

- **"Get the Big Picture."** Be aware of the whole traffic scene. This is the process of putting together all of the data compiled from "aiming high" and "keeping your eyes moving."

- **"Leave Yourself an Out."** Avoid being "boxed in." Always keep a cushion around your vehicle. This requires constant adjustments to traffic conditions.

- **"Make Sure They See You."** Avoid surprising other drivers by making yourself as visible as possible and by making your maneuvers predictable.

A second system is **S.I.P.D.E.** That stands for Search, Identify, Predict, Decide and Execute. It is a method of gathering sensory information in order to develop a complete and accurate picture of the driving situation.

- **Search**—Conduct a systematic search of the driving environment. This enables you to perceive possible situations ahead, behind and on both sides of your vehicle. You do this by following a few steps.

  —**Keep your primary focus on your current path of travel.** You must always be aware of what is directly in front of you.

  —**Scan the traffic scene.** Look for things that could affect you by scanning the roadway, traffic (both vehicular and foot), fixed objects and the weather conditions. Use rapid eye movements to avoid fixating on individual objects.

  —**Check mirrors and instruments.** Use the interior and exterior mirrors to see what is behind you and to your side. Periodically glance at the instrument panel for speed control.

  —**Anticipate visual lead time.** Listen for audible clues when your line-of-sight is limited. This may allow you to identify potential obstacles before you see them.

- **Identify**—Condition yourself to spot possible hazardous factors or situations.

- **Predict**—Forecast what could happen if conditions continue to develop. You do this by relating the present situation with past experiences and knowledge. Over time, you develop an ability to recognize immediate and potential hazards as well as evaluating risks.

- **Decide**—Once you have predicted what will happen, come up with a course of action to take.

- **Execute**—Carry out your decision, utilizing your driving skills to maintain the safety of your vehicle and you.

The third system is the **Zone Control System**. This is a three-step process which gives guidelines for how and where a driver should search, what to search for and what to do when a deteriorating situation is identified. The steps are as follows:

- **Step A—See the zone change to your path of travel and to your line of sight.** This includes searching ahead and to the sides as well as checking mirrors and blind spots frequently.

- **Step B—Evaluate other zones to determine your options.** Always expect the unexpected and be ready to react safely.

- **Step C—Get optimum control using speed control, lane positioning and communications.** Speed control is choosing between maintaining, increasing or decreasing your current speed. Lane position involves moving your vehicle to the portion of your lane that provides the most safety. Communicating with other drivers helps eliminate surprises. Means of communication include using headlights, brake lights, turn signals, hand signals, horns, and emergency lights and sirens. The position of your vehicle on the road and the speed that you are traveling can also communicate your intentions to other drivers.

Occupant Protection Devices

Another key component of emergency vehicle operations is **officer survival**. You are much more likely to be involved in a crash than the average driver. You spend more time behind the wheel of a car and are forced to drive in varying conditions and occasionally under extreme stress. It should be no surprise that **motor vehicle collisions are the leading cause of injury and disability to peace officers.** Approximately twenty-five percent of officer fatalities in the line of duty are traffic related. You must protect yourself by taking advantage of the safety features in your vehicle.

Occupant protection devices can be divided into two categories: active and passive. The active devices are the ones that require some action on your part to use them. The most important of these is the **safety belt**. A safety belt reduces the chance of injury and death in several ways.

How a Safety Belt Protects You

- **Redistributes crash forces.** It protects your most vulnerable areas by shifting dangerous forces to areas strong enough to absorb them. If all people wore safety belts, the number of serious injuries and fatalities would be reduced by about fifty percent.

- **Prevents you from striking the steering wheel, windshield, interior post or dashboard.** It also keeps you from being knocked into equipment. This is critical when you consider the extra items carried by an emergency vehicle, such as radios, shotguns, batons, flashlights, computers, spotlights and radars.

- **Helps you to remain behind the wheel.** This gives you a better chance to control your vehicle after the collision. It also prevents you from being ejected from the car. If you are ejected, the chance of being seriously injured or killed increases dramatically.

Some officers also feel that a safety belt causes problems. Two common myths are that a belt can trap you in the car and that uncoupling it takes too much time in critical moments. With a little practice, however, you will find that using a safety belt does not interfere with your job. Given its positive impact on officer survival, a safety belt is worth the extra two or three seconds that it adds to entering and exiting your vehicle.

To be effective, a safety belt must be properly adjusted. It should be worn low on the hips and extend over the shoulder. It should also be snug. If the belt has too much slack, it may not prevent you from hitting the steering wheel or windshield during a collision. The illustration below shows the proper way to wear a safety belt as well as some of the common mistakes.

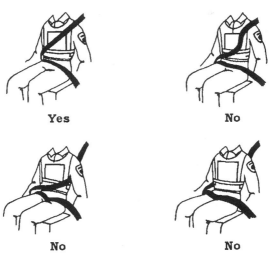

Yes   No

No   No

If the safety considerations do not convince you to wear a safety belt, maybe the legal ones will. In the areas that have safety belt laws, exceptions are rarely made for public safety officers. You have to use a safety belt in order to comply with state statutes and agency policy. In fact, not wearing one can cost you dearly. Recent court decisions have held that officers injured because they failed to use available safety belts may lose their workmen's compensation or other benefits.

Another active safety device is the **head restraint**. This protects your neck from whiplash. When adjusting it, set the head restraint at a height that equals the middle of your head, level with the ears.

Door locks help keep the doors secure during a collision. This reduces the chance of you being ejected. Also, doors that do not pop open help maintain your vehicle's structural integrity during a rollover, thereby reducing the chance of the roof collapsing. You should keep the doors locked at all times.

There are other active safety measures you can take as well. Wearing body armor reduces the chance of chest injuries. Also, keep loose equipment such as shotguns, flashlights and batons securely stowed. This helps prevent those items from flying about in the event of a sudden stop or collision.

Passive Safety Components

Passive safety components are the devices and features that do not require any action on your part. One of the best is the **air bag**, which inflates at the moment of impact and acts as a pillow for a person being thrown forward. This cushioning effect allows you to withstand a much more serious collision than you could otherwise.

It is important that you understand that an air bag is designed to work with safety belts, not replace them. It does have limitations.

Limitations of an Air Bag

- Will not protect you against secondary collisions. They deflate immediately after the initial impact.
- Cannot prevent you from being ejected.
- Does not open at side impacts.

An air bag is a wonderful safety feature that has saved many lives. But nothing will protect you more than wearing a safety belt.

Most vehicle designs include other passive safety features. These often include collapsible steering columns, padded dashboards and door panels, recessed knobs and door handles, and windshields that help prevent flying glass. If you are aware of the features that your vehicle offers and know how to maximize their use, you reduce the risks you are exposed to each day. Any edge in your favor may make the difference between walking away from an accident and ending up in the hospital.

Review Questions

1. What are the three components of driving?

2. Why is driving an emergency vehicle more dangerous than a normal street vehicle?

3. If your agency advocates a specific driving system, list each component and explain how each works within the system.

Six

The Human Factor

Objectives

After completing this chapter, you will be able to

- *Identify several dangerous attitudes*
- *Outline the steps for building a positive attitude*
- *Understand the physical challenges of emergency vehicle operations*
- *Take steps to maintain good physical condition*
- *List the rules that affect controlled substances and driving*

While an emergency vehicle is a sophisticated piece of equipment, it is really nothing more than a tool. As with any other tool, you are the one who makes it work properly and safely. To maximize your vehicle's effectiveness, you personally need to be in good shape, both mentally and physically.

Emotions and Attitudes

Emotions such as fear, love, hate, surprise, joy and excitement affect the part of the brain that controls thought, reason and judgment. Strong emotions can affect you physically, causing your heart to beat faster, your face to flush, muscles to tense, and an increase in respiratory and blood pressure rates. Repeated extreme emotions can lead to long-term health problems such as ulcers and changes in appetite and digestive processes.

It should be no surprise that emotions have a profound impact on behavior in general and vehicle operations in particular. In one sense, emotions can be a positive force. Love of family and friends, a desire to be successful, and a fear of legal liability can result in safe driving habits. On the other hand, negative emotions can cause distorted interpretations of events, faulty judgment and a reduced ability to perform precision skills.

Attitudes also have a profound effect on behaviors. When we think of someone as having a bad attitude, we usually picture him or her as having a "chip on the shoulder." However, a person does not have to be angry or uncooperative to be in a hazardous frame of mind. There are several different types of problem attitudes; some of which are very subtle. It is possible that you might exhibit a problem attitude and not even know it. Several dangerous attitudes and their signs are presented here.

- **Overconfidence**—Officers who are overconfident frequently take unnecessary risks and exceed their limitations. This reckless behavior has contributed to the deaths of thousands of drivers and passengers. Signs include:
  —"Showing off" your driving ability
  —A feeling of invincibility and believing that the possibility of death or injury does not exist for you
  —A tendency to make statements such as "It won't happen to me," "Only less-experienced drivers get into collisions," and "No one ever gets away from me"

- **Lack of confidence**—This is just as dangerous as overconfidence. If you lack confidence, you frequently make bad decisions or no decision at all. That results in an inability to respond safely to the various situations that confront you. Signs include:
  —A feeling of fear when attempting a maneuver
  —Insecurity resulting from inexperience or previous mishaps
  —Anxiety symptoms such as profuse sweating and hands tightly gripping the steering wheel

- **Self-righteousness**—Self-righteous officers tend to think that they are above the law and are never wrong. That leads them to take unnecessary risks. It also inhibits the acceptance of constructive criticism, making it impossible to improve their professional skills. When you combine self-righteousness with another attitude such as over-confidence, you end up with an extremely dangerous mix. Signs include:
  —Certainty that you are always right
  —Tendency to think that the law applies to others but not to you
  —Believing that everyone will get out of your way because you are a law enforcement officer

- **Impatience**—Impatient officers frequently act without thinking about the consequences. This often leads to viewing normal vehicular tasks as obstacles and other drivers as adversaries. This usually results in dangerous tendencies such as excessive speed for conditions, unsafe passing, illegal and unsafe turns, following too closely, unsafe backing and abuse of equipment. Signs include:
  —The feeling that you are always in a hurry
  —The belief that others are preventing you from getting where you want to go
  —A strong tendency to do more than one thing at a time
  —Constant facial and body tension
  —Frequently hurrying or interrupting the speech of others

- **Preoccupation**—When you are preoccupied, you have a tendency to think about things other than vehicle operations. It frequently stems from boredom, letting personal problems spill over into your professional life, or the lingering effects of an emotionally charged call. Preoccupation leads to carelessness. A distracted mind does not register images as quickly as an attentive one. Defensive driving techniques are often forgotten or poorly performed when you are not focused. Signs include:

—Your mind constantly wandering to things other than the task at hand

—Doing other things while operating a vehicle, such as eating, drinking or smoking

Willingness to Improve

You must not let negative emotions and attitudes lead you to ake high-risk actions. Training programs can help you turn high-'isk actions into low-risk habits, but the key to success is you. You must be willing to improve. If you are, the following steps will help you become a safe, effective vehicle operator who is an ısset for both the community and the agency.

Rules for Developing Good Driving Habits

- **Use training to improve your skills.** Training builds confidence. When you have been well-trained, you know you have the skills needed to handle almost any situation. Training also helps you understand the state laws and agency policies that apply to all phases of emergency vehicle operations. Acting within the law prevents self-righteousness and increases respect for other drivers.

- **Practice what you learn in training**. This forces you to think about what you are doing. If you are focused, you cannot be preoccupied. Always thinking about and evaluating your options will make you a more patient driver. And with constant practice, you can determine what you can and cannot do. Knowing that will help you keep from becoming an overconfident driver.

- **Trust your judgment.** Once your trained skills become second nature, you develop a sense about what to do in almost every situation. In most cases, your "gut feeling" will be the correct procedure and will help prevent you from taking unnecessary chances.

The Physical Challenge of Vehicle Operations

You need more than controlled emotions and a good attitude to drive an emergency vehicle. You have to be in good physical shape as well. Your senses must function properly to identify potential hazards and make a proper decision. You then need good motor skills to implement that decision correctly and safely.

Maintaining good physical condition is a challenge because the factors that affect your health can impact you during one shift or over the course of several days, weeks or months. One such factor is **fatigue.** Officers who are tired often become irritable and discourteous, causing them to overreact to minor irritations. More important, fatigue affects vision efficiency and tends to lengthen perception, decision and reaction times.

Fatigue is common among law enforcement officers because of the long hours sitting inside their vehicles. On some shifts, you may spend more time than normal behind the wheel of your patrol car. In addition, you might be on a late-night shift when you are accustomed to working days. If your body thinks it should be asleep, fatigue can easily set in. A couple things you can do to minimize the effects of fatigue are listed below.

Steps for Avoiding Fatigue

- **Get proper rest and exercise.** A well-maintained body needs less rest than one that is constantly overtaxed due to poor physical condition.

- **Keep fresh air circulating through the vehicle.** One way is to keep a window slightly open while driving. Another is to always have your fresh air vents open.

A long-term factor that can affect your physical condition is stress. The nature of law enforcement work subjects you to highly stressful situations. These situations usually occur without warning and may be preceded by a period of relative inactivity.

Some stress is good. An shot of adrenaline can increase your physical performance. You may become more aware of your surroundings and be able to think more clearly. It does have a cumulative effect, however. Stress increases your blood pressure and causes irregular breathing. Prolonged stress may impair rational thought. When you reach that threshold, your ability to perform effectively decreases rapidly.

Steps for Controlling Stress

- **Talk to someone you trust.** Getting problems off your chest helps keep your emotions from building up inside you.

- **Do not take your work home with you.** When your shift is over, pamper yourself. Turn your attention to some other activities or simply relax. You should not dwell on work-related issues and problems twenty-four hours a day.

- **Stay physically fit.** Just fifteen to thirty minutes a day of flexibility and cardiovascular exercises helps reduce the effects of stress. An added benefit is that regular exercise increases your physical capabilities.

The Dangers of Substance Abuse

Consumption of alcohol or drugs before or during a shift is a prescription for disaster. Your performance will be dangerously affected by any controlled substance, be it beer, liquor, wine, an illegal narcotic or even medication prescribed by a doctor. Controlled substances can be divided into two groups: depressants and stimulants.

Depressants are drugs that lower blood pressure, reduce mental processing and slow motor reaction responses. They are used to reduce pain and produce "good feelings." Alcohol is the most widely used and abused drug in this category. Other depressants include tranquilizers, relaxants and antihistamines.

Stimulants get their name because they stimulate the central nervous system and produce increased alertness and energy. People commonly use them for appetite suppression, fatigue reduction, and mood elevation. Unfortunately, they often result in anxiety and drastic mood swings. Common stimulants are amphetamines, caffeine and nicotine.

Every officer knows about the dangers of drugs and alcohol, especially when it comes to driving. However, the use of controlled substances is very common. Some are extremely mild and are ingested from seemingly innocent sources, such as coffee and soda pop. Operating a vehicle while under the effect of any controlled substance, no matter how mild, can have dangerous consequences. You need to know the rules for when you can and cannot get behind the wheel of a patrol car.

Rules for Drug Usage and Vehicle Operations

- **Never drive when under the influence of alcohol.** Bear in mind that people with hangovers are still under the influence and are not capable of functioning normally.

- **Drink coffee and smoke in moderation.** Caffeine and nicotine are stimulants. If you find that you are having side effects, such as nervousness, then do not drive. On a related note, avoid drinking or smoking while driving. Spilling hot coffee or dropping a cigarette ash into your lap will certainly be a distraction. Smoking also affects visual acuity and depth perception.

- **Find out the side effects of prescription drugs.** Your physician and druggist can inform you how a drug will affect your driving ability. Read the labels and instructions carefully. If they warn you not to operate a motor vehicle, then don't.

- **Understand the impact of an illness being treated with medication.** Taking prescription or over-the-counter drugs is an indication that you are not at your best. Some health conditions are serious enough to prohibit driving, even if they are being successfully treated.

Review Questions

1. List five of the common dangerous attitudes and give some of the signs of each.

2. What are the steps for overcoming dangerous attitudes?

3. What steps can you take to avoid fatigue?

4. How can you control stress?

5. List some of the common everyday products that are agents of controlled substances.

6. What are the rules for driving while under the effect of a controlled substance?

Seven

Maintaining Top Vehicle Performance

Objectives

After completing this chapter, you will be able to

- *Identify negative behaviors that lead to malfunctions*
- *Perform a complete vehicle inspection*
- *Identify what to do in the event of a mechanical failure*

Law enforcement activities are hard on emergency vehicles. However, with proper care and maintenance, your patrol car will more than likely meet the demands placed on it. Of course, to reach that goal, your cooperation is essential.

Vehicle Performance Begins with the Right Attitude

One reason why many emergency vehicles break down is that officers do not always drive with proper care. Some officers adopt the attitude that it is acceptable to abuse a law enforcement vehicle because "it's not my car." That attitude is unprofessional and can shorten the life and effectiveness of a vehicle.

Behaviors Leading to Vehicle Breakdown

- Driving over speed bumps, curbs or railroad tracks at high speeds

- Overworking the brakes
- Resting the left foot on the brake pedal
- Idling too long, especially in hot weather
- Over-revving the engine
- Downshifting at high speeds and shifting from drive to reverse while still moving
- Putting the vehicle in park while it is still in motion

You should drive an emergency vehicle as if it were your personal car. Abusing your patrol car is expensive. It costs your agency money and it may cost you, too. Vehicle abuse may subject you to disciplinary action.

An unprofessional attitude is also dangerous. Your emergency vehicle is your most important piece of equipment. Compare it with your handgun. Both are instruments of lethal force and both can save your life. But consider how often you use each of them. Your handgun is rarely used, but you use your patrol car almost non-stop every day.

Drive your emergency vehicle as if your life depends on it. It does.

Vehicle Inspection

An emergency vehicle should be inspected before each patrol. An inspection accomplishes two important goals. First, it helps maintain operational efficiency and safety of the vehicle. When you actively look for mechanical problems, the chance of a vehicle malfunction is almost completely eliminated.

Second, an inspection builds your confidence in your car. There is no way to really know what happened to your vehicle during the shift before yours. If it passes your own evaluation, however, you know that you will be able to accomplish almost any objective, be it reaching a call destination or assisting a fellow officer in need.

Many departments have their own vehicle inspection procedure. If yours does not, you can develop a systematic sequence that covers the three basic areas.

1. Mechanical
—Fluids (brake, oil, transmission, radiator, battery, windshield wiper, and power steering)
—Belts and hoses
—Wires

2. Exterior
—Tires (air pressure and tread)
—Mirrors
—Windshield and windows
—All lights (headlights, taillights, emergency lights and spotlight)
—Hood and door latches
—Any external damage

3. Interior
—Brakes and emergency brake
—Horn, P.A. system and sirens
—Gauges and warning devices, especially fuel gauge
—Windshield wipers
—Occupant protection systems
—Mirrors
—Door locks
—Seat adjustment and security

Following the same procedure every time will enable you to complete a detailed inspection within a few minutes. If your inspection turns up a problem, report it immediately. Too many officers ignore maintenance needs. This ultimately leads to increased costs of vehicle operations. Even worse, it jeopardizes your safety and that of your fellow officers and the public you have sworn to protect.

When reporting damage, do not rely on oral communication. Write down what is wrong and report it before you begin your shift. That way, you cannot be falsely accused of causing any damage.

Reacting to a Sudden Mechanical Failure

As stated earlier, a thorough inspection and maintenance program almost completely eliminates the possibility of a mechanical failure. However, no matter how well maintained your vehicle is, there is always a chance that something will go wrong. Should you experience a sudden mechanical failure, there are three simple steps to follow, no matter what the problem is.

Steps to Take in the Event of a Mechanical Failure

1. Slow down.
2. Get off the road and stop. Signal your intentions as you move out of traffic, and turn on your hazard lights once you have stopped.
3. Use your radio to call in for advice and assistance.

Review Questions

1. Why is an unprofessional attitude towards an emergency vehicle dangerous?

2. What are the two objectives of a vehicle inspection?

3. What is your agency's practice when it comes to inspecting vehicles?

4. Why should you immediately report any damage found in an inspection? Why do damage reports need to be written, instead of transmitted orally?

5. What three steps should you take in the event of a sudden mechanical failure?

Eight

Basic Vehicle Operations

Objectives

After completing this chapter, you will be able to

- *Outline the basic components of operating a vehicle in a non-emergency mode*
- *Explain the impact of an anti-lock braking system*
- *Establish a safe following distance*
- *Use your radio effectively and safely*

Up to this point, we have discussed many of the conceptual issues of emergency vehicle operations. Now it is time to cover the basic skills needed to control your vehicle. These are the skills that allow you to do your job and prevent potential collisions from becoming real ones.

Speed Control

Speed is controlled by acceleration and deceleration. The degree to which you accelerate or decelerate should be based on three criteria. First is engine power and responsiveness. Second are traction conditions such as whether the roadway is dry or wet and whether material under the tires could affect a sudden increase in speed. Third are roadway characteristics and design. These include whether the road is level, uphill or downhill, and whether the road is straight or curving. With these three criteria in mind, you should follow two rules for speed control.

Rules for Speed Control

- **Acceleration should always be smooth.** Never stomp on the accelerator, even if a high rate of speed is needed. That might cause the wheels to spin, reducing traction and possibly causing a skid.

- **Acceleration should be in direct relationship to your intended path of travel.** You can accelerate faster when you are moving in the direction you want to go.

The same rules apply to deceleration, although your intended path of travel does not impact deceleration as much as it does acceleration. The smoothest way to slow down is to simply take your foot off of the accelerator. Another method of deceleration is braking.

Braking

The ability to brake safely is determined primarily by your speed and the available stopping distance. Obviously, the faster you are going, the more distance you need to bring your vehicle to a stop. A number of other factors also have an impact. Driver-related factors include perception, reaction time, physical condition, emotional state and attitude. Environmental factors include road surface as well as road and weather conditions. The condition of the brakes themselves and the vehicle in general also affect your ability to stop.

Given all the variables, it is not surprising that everyone does not agree on exact stopping distances. The chart on the following page estimates the amount of space needed to stop at thirty, forty and fifty miles per hour. These estimates are based on an alert driver searching ahead at acceptable distances and reacting within the normal ranges of time. They assume that the vehicle, brakes and tires are in good working order. They also assume that the pavement is dry and level. Keep in mind that these figures are not exact; they are simply averages used for illustration.

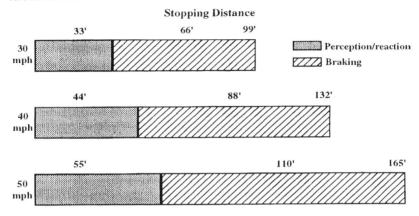

There are two categories of stops. The first is a **controlled stop**. It should be used whenever you have enough distance for a smooth deceleration. For this, you can use two types of braking. **"Early and smooth"** is the application of brake pressure early, with a smooth release of the brakes as the vehicle slows to a complete stop. **"Pumping,"** also known as **"stab and jab,"** is applying and releasing the brakes over and over until the vehicle comes to a stop.

The second category is a **sudden stop**. This is where you are forced to stop quickly in the shortest possible distance. If your vehicle is equipped with an **antilock braking system (ABS)**, which most are, you can depress the brake pedal hard and hold it down as far as it will go. The ABS prevents the wheels from locking up. This enables you to maintain control of your vehicle while stopping in short distances.

Regardless of what kind of stop you have to make, there are a few rules you should follow when braking.

Rules for Braking

- **Avoid left foot braking.** That often leads to riding the brakes. Constant pressure causes the brakes to heat up and lose their ability to grab the wheels properly.

This is known as brake fade. In addition, riding the brakes keeps your brake lights illuminated, sending confusing messages to vehicles behind you.

- **Use the upper half of your right foot to apply pressure on the brake pedal.** Keep your heel on the floor. To increase pressure, pivot on your heel rather than moving your foot. This gives you greater sensitivity on the pedal and requires less exertion.

- **Do not stare at the front hood of your vehicle while braking.** Check both your sides for a path of escape if needed. Look to the rear to avoid being hit from behind. Also, search ten to twelve seconds ahead to see if the conditions which forced your braking actions have changed.

Steering

Steering combines hand positioning with hand movement. When backing up, one hand should be at the twelve o'clock position on the steering wheel and your body turned so you can look in the direction your vehicle is moving. Backing up is discussed in detail in the chapter on high-risk maneuvers.

When your vehicle is moving forward, keeping two hands on the steering wheel allows for quick steering needs and helps you balance out the resulting vehicle weight transfers. It also provides quick access to dashboard items.

The ideal hand positions are nine o'clock-three o'clock or ten o'clock-two o'clock on the steering wheel. The nine-three position is recommended for urban driving where speeds are generally under forty-five miles per hour and steering inputs are more frequent. The ten-two position is recommended for rural or highway driving where speeds exceed forty-five and steering inputs are less frequent. Regardless of which position is used, you should apply light pressure with your fingers and heavier pressure with your thumbs.

When your hands are in the proper position, you can react to any steering need by using one of the three acceptable methods. **Shuffle steering** is sliding your hands on the wheel in small increments. This lets you avoid getting your hands tangled from crossing one over the other. It is best for gradual turns where you do not need to react quickly.

Hand-over-hand is using one hand to turn the wheel as far as possible while crossing the bottom hand to the top. This allows for a rapid and continual steering maneuver. Hand-over-hand works well for sharp turns and skid control. **Evasive steering** is turning the steering wheel one-half rotation in one direction, a full rotation in the opposite direction, and then returning back to the original position.

Regardless of which method you employ, there are a couple of rules to follow when making a steering adjustment.

Rules for Steering

- **Steering inputs should be smooth.** Abrupt steering changes often result in sudden weight transfers, which can throw a vehicle into a skid. Overcorrecting the initial transfer may cause a strong weight shift back in the opposite direction. That, too, can lead to a skid.

- **Concentrate your sight on the desired path of travel.** Most drivers steer in the direction they are looking.

Cornering

On every tour of duty, you are likely to encounter all sorts of corners, ranging from turns at residential intersections to curves on superhighways. No matter where a corner is located, it has three critical points. First is the **entry**. When approaching the entry, slow down and position your vehicle to get a good look at the curve and the best angle for negotiating it. In most cases, the best entry position is the outermost position in your lane. This makes the turn wider and allows for a faster cornering speed.

The second point is the **apex**. The apex is the area where your vehicle comes closest to the inside or tight portion of the roadway. More specifically, it is the point where you can begin to steer your vehicle out of the corner.

Since all turns are not ninety-degree turns, the apex is not always at the center of a corner. The severity of the curve determines the apex. If the severity of the curve eases as you move through it, the apex will be earlier. If the curve gets sharper, the apex will be later. Selecting the proper apex makes the distance that you must travel as short as possible.

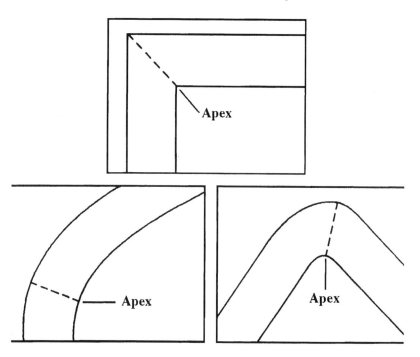

It is important that you understand that the true apex of a corner may not be the safest one. You must always **take the best apex for the available roadway**. For instance, when cornering to the left, you may have to take a higher apex. This is especially important on a two-lane road or highway, where you may encounter traffic coming in the opposite direction. The higher apex prevents you from cutting the curve or turning so sharply that you cross into another vehicle's path of travel.

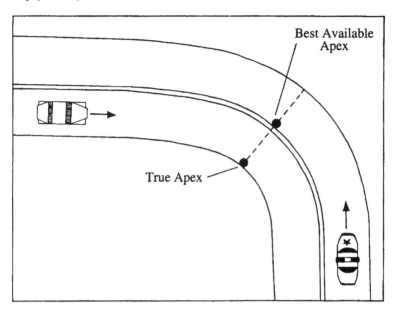

The last point of every corner is the **exit**. This is where you position your vehicle to take a new path of travel as it leaves the corner. As your steering inputs decrease, you can safely speed up. To safely negotiate all turns and curves, you should use a precise, step-by-step system of cornering.

Steps for Cornering

- **Evaluate the corner by searching ten to twelve seconds ahead.** If you are making a turn at an intersection, evaluate both your present path of travel and the one you intend to take after completing the turn.

- **Use your turn signals when turning right or left.** Also check your mirrors and blind spots for traffic that might be affected as you make the turn.

- **Position your vehicle for cornering.** Right turns should be from right lanes; left turns from left lanes. If you are on a highway or road, enter the curve from the outside portion of your lane. However, do not swerve into another vehicle's path of travel, especially if it's one of oncoming traffic.

- **Establish the proper speed before entering the turn or curve.** Braking in a corner reduces your steering control. If you need to slow down, do so before you get to the turn or curve. Also, be prepared to yield to any oncoming traffic or pedestrians when making a turn at an intersection.

- **Steer for the apex as you enter the corner.** Make sure your path to the apex does not interfere with other traffic. Avoid steering with only one hand. Do not make any aggressive movements. Even if you are travelling at a safe speed, a sudden steering input can throw a vehicle into a skid.

- **As you clear the apex, steer toward the desired exit position.** You can also begin to increase your speed once you reach the apex.

Maintaining an Acceptable Following Distance

There are two major reasons why following distance is critical for emergency vehicles. First, many drivers overreact to seeing a patrol car approaching. The most common response is a quick, unexpected braking action. This increases the rate of closure.

Second, as an officer on patrol, you must keep an eye on the environment around you. This includes other vehicles, pedestrians and buildings. This surveillance often distracts you from seeing what is directly in front of you. If another car stops suddenly, you could easily run into the back of it.

You can reduce the chance of a collision by maintaining a **safe following distance**. This is measured in seconds. Some law enforcement agencies recommend a two-second distance for routine driving; others advocate a four-second gap. Most require a distance of at least four seconds at higher speeds. You establish your following distance by using a simple procedure.

Steps for Establishing Your Following Distance

1. **Find a fixed marker that the vehicle in front of you is about to pass.** It can be anything that is not moving, such as a traffic sign or mileage marker.

2. **Start counting as soon as its rear bumper clears the mark.** Say the numbers "1001, 1002" and so on until the front of your vehicle reaches the mark. Each number represents one second. If you get to the fixed marker at 1004, you are four seconds away.

By repeating this process frequently, you develop a sense for how far you can travel in four seconds at various speeds. Then it becomes easy to maintain a sufficient cushion between other motorists and you.

If you are driving in **heavy congestion**, an acceptable following distance cannot always be maintained. The sheer volume of traffic prevents you from keeping four seconds behind the car in front of you. If you try to, another vehicle will likely move into the gap and take away your safety cushion.

Just because you are in heavy traffic does not mean that you cannot protect yourself. There are several steps you can take to increase your safety.

Rules for Driving in Heavy Congestion

- **Avoid driving in and out of lanes.** Try to find a lane where traffic is moving smoothly. If you find one, stay there.

- **Leave yourself a path of escape.** Avoid getting boxed in by traffic.

- **Increase your visibility to other drivers.** Do not travel in other vehicle's blind spots.

In general, your best course of action is to drive with the flow of traffic. Unless you are on an emergency run, the same rules that apply to other motorists apply to you. Even during an emergency, you are still obligated to drive in a manner that does not endanger the public.

Using Your Radio

As a law enforcement officer, you need to maintain constant communication while on patrol. If you have a partner, your partner should use the radio while you concentrate on driving. However, if you are alone in your vehicle, you must use the radio without putting yourself at risk.

The best time for radio usage is when your vehicle is stopped. If you are not moving, you do not have to worry about controlling your car while you talk. However, you are frequently required to respond to a radio transmission while your vehicle is in motion.

Rules for Radio Usage while Driving

- **Use the radio when visibility is best.** If you can search forward and to the sides, you are more likely to spot something approaching that might make radio usage dangerous. Also, officers tend to steer towards communication equipment during use. If you are on a flat, straight road, you usually have a greater margin for safe steering adjustments.

- **Avoid transmitting while going through corners and curves.** Using the radio while making a turn forces you to steer with one hand. Besides reducing vehicle control, you run the risk of wrapping the microphone cord around the steering wheel assembly. It is better to wait until you come out of the turn before responding to questions or comments.

- **Speak clearly and efficiently.** Avoid time-consuming conversations. Know the correct radio codes, language, street names and locations. This enables you to transmit and receive messages in the shortest amount of time and with a minimal amount of distractions to your driving function. Also, keep the windows closed to reduce sound distractions.

- **Secure the microphone in a consistent location.** This enables you to locate the microphone at any time without having to search for it. It also allows you to store it quickly.

Review Questions

1. What are the rules for controlling speed?

2. What are the three points in every turn and corner?

3. What does your agency consider to be a safe following distance behind another vehicle? How do you determine your following distance?

4. What three safety steps should you take when driving in heavy traffic?

5. If you must use your radio while your vehicle is in motion, what steps should you take to maintain your safety?

Nine

The High-Risk Maneuvers

Objectives

After completing this chapter, you will be able to

- *Identify the maneuvers that frequently contribute to collisions*
- *Develop strategies for handling these maneuvers*

Many of the collisions that occur in normal vehicle operations take place while performing basic everyday maneuvers. However, if you know what these high-risk maneuvers are and how to execute them properly, you dramatically reduce the chance of an accident.

Backing

A high percentage of non-emergency collisions occur while vehicles are moving in reverse. There are several reasons why backing up is so difficult. First, visibility is often limited when you have to look over your shoulder to see out the rear window. Second, the effects of your steering inputs are more exaggerated when going backwards.

The main cause of backing accidents, however, is carelessness. You have to know what is behind you before your vehicle starts moving. In addition, some officers forget to take into account that emergency vehicles are often larger than personal cars. You can reduce the risk of driving in reverse if you follow a few simple rules.

Rules for Backing

- **Position your hands properly.** To back in a straight line or turn to the right, put your left hand at the twelve o'clock position on the wheel; drape your right arm over the front seat for support. To turn to the left, keep both hands on the wheel. That will give you more control.

- **Sound your horn before you start.** This draws attention to your vehicle so people can be alert to your presence as you back up. In this manner, sounding your horn is similar to the beeping sound that many commercial vehicles make when they are moving in reverse.

- **Look out the rear window by turning your body.** Look over your right shoulder for right turns and over your left shoulder for left turns.

- **Accelerate slowly.** The faster you go, the harder it will be to maintain control. In close quarters, keep your vehicle in a creeping mode.

- **Keep hand movements to a minimum.** Turn the steering wheel with a firm control. Frequently check the front corners to make sure that their path is clear of obstructions.

Collisions frequently result from going in and out of parking spaces. There is a proper way to park your vehicle in each of the three main types of spaces: stall, parallel and perpendicular. The diagrams on the following page illustrate the correct techniques for each.

It is a good idea to plan for your exit as you park your vehicle. This is especially true when perpendicular parking. Whenever you are perpendicular parking, try to back into the space. That way, you are able to exit quicker and with more control if you have to respond to an emergency.

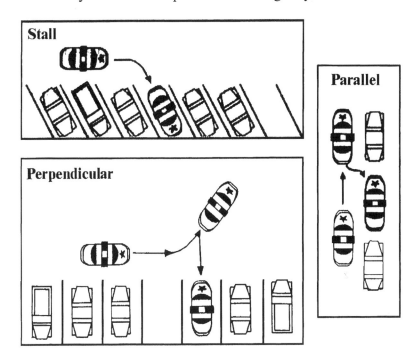

Turns and Turnabouts

Many collisions occur during right and left turns. However, if you practice a system for making turns, you can develop a habit that minimizes the chances of an accident. One method for making turns is listed below.

Steps for Making a Turn

1. Get your vehicular speed under control.
2. Signal your intentions.
3. Check mirrors and blind spots.
4. Position your vehicle on the proper side of the roadway. Left turns should be from the left lane; right turns should be from the right lane.

5. Scan the intersection to make sure the new path-of-travel is clear.
6. Maintain proper tracking control. Keep the brakes applied until halfway through the turn and use the hand-over-hand or shuffle steering technique.
7. Accelerate after the turn.

Turnabouts are high-risk maneuvers because you have to cross over lanes of traffic. Check your agency's policy regarding turnabouts. Some agencies prohibit turnabouts. Others have guidelines on when you can and cannot turn around on a public roadway. If there is no departmental policy for turns, use the procedures discussed below. However, keep in mind that turnabouts are dangerous procedures. You should be trained on their use and you should practice them in a controlled environment before employing them on the street.

A **"U" turn** is turning your car around 180 degrees without stopping. Before performing a "U" turn, slow down and pull to the extreme right of the lane or shoulder. Be sure to use your turn signals to indicate your intention, and do not accelerate until you have completed the turn.

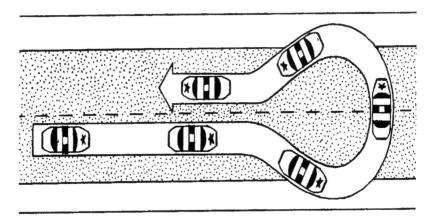

If the road is too narrow for a complete "U" turn, you can make a **three-point turn** or a broken "U" turn, as shown on the next page. Here you turn as far as you can and then back up to give yourself the space you need to complete the maneuver. Keep the distance you drive in reverse at a minimum.

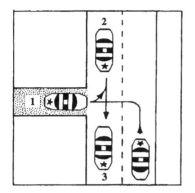 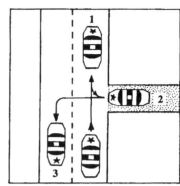

For a right-hand turn, utilize an adjacent road or a driveway. Back into the road or driveway and then drive out front first. Be sure to check the roadway for traffic and pedestrians before and during the maneuver.

Changing Lanes

When you change lanes, you often merge into another vehicle's path of travel. Most people involved in collisions while changing lanes simply dart in and out of traffic with little regard for other vehicles. And they often gain very little in terms of time or advantage over other drivers.

Before changing lanes, ask yourself two questions. First, is the lane change necessary? Second, what will I gain by doing it? If you decide to make a change, be sure you do it safely.

Steps for Changing Lanes

1. **Check the adjacent lane for a clear path.** Use your mirrors to find an opening.

2. **Indicate your intention with your turn signal.** The signal should be on for at least three seconds before initiating the change.

3. **Confirm the opening.** Check your mirrors again. Glance over your shoulder to check your blind spot.

4. **Use a slight turn of the steering wheel.** This gives you a smooth, gradual movement. Time your merge into the adjacent lane so you do not interfere with other traffic. This may require an increase in speed.

Passing Slower Vehicles

Passing a slower vehicle may be the most dangerous situation that you encounter in a non-emergency mode. The problem is that motorists are unpredictable, especially when they see a law enforcement vehicle approaching them. Slow drivers often slow down even more. This makes your closure time even less. In addition, it is difficult to accurately judge the speed of traffic approaching from the other direction. So you may not have as much time for passing as you first thought.

Steps for Passing Slower Vehicles

1. **Look for the best passing location.** Be sure that everything is all clear. Check ahead, behind, the sides and your blind spots.

2. **Signal your intention to pass.** If crossing into lanes of oncoming traffic, turn on your low-beam headlights to increase your vehicle's visibility.

3. **Accelerate smoothly and quickly.** Pass to the left of the vehicle, staying as far away as possible for the best visibility and separation.

4. **Keep searching for changes in the traffic conditions.** Have escape options planned in case of a sudden need. This is especially critical if you are passing more than one vehicle at a time.

5. **Move back to your original lane.** When you can see the headlights of the passed vehicle in your rear view mirror, you will have enough room to return to your lane safely. Again, signal your intention with your turn indicator.

Driving Too Fast for Conditions

You must always be aware of your speed, especially when operating in a non-emergency mode. As mentioned in the chapter on lawsuits, most state statutes permit law enforcement vehicles to exceed the speed limit only when responding to an emergency. There are occasions, however, when even the posted speed limit can be too fast.

The speed limit assumes that you are in an ideal traffic environment for that particular area. If your line-of-sight is restricted, you have less time to perceive and react to potential problems. So while your speed may be appropriate for a clear path of travel, it may be too fast when visibility is limited.

Since law enforcement officers are more prone to liability proceedings than normal drivers, you must be aware of the areas of risk. Collision data indicates that accidents due to limited visibility occur most often in four areas: intersections, hills, curves, and behind slower traffic.

Whenever you cannot adequately see ahead, you must assume an obstacle exists that must be accounted for. Following a few prudent rules will increase your safety as well as the safety of the general public.

Rules to Follow if Your Line-of-Sight Is Restricted

- **Get the best speed control.** Take your foot off of the accelerator and cover the brake.

- **Keep your following distance.** Also look behind you for traffic coming from the rear and traveling in your blind spots.

- **Check ahead for possible escape paths.** By preparing to move away from a potential problem, you often decrease the angle and severity of a steering response, if one is needed.

Controlling a Skid

All too often, drivers believe a skid happens only in bad weather or at a high speed, but that is not the case. A skid can occur at any time, during any driving situation.

There are three common types of skids. A **braking skid** occurs when one or more brakes lock up, usually the result of a driver braking late or too hard. Fortunately, vehicles equipped with anti-lock brakes cannot get into braking skids unless the ABS is malfunctioning.

A **cornering skid** takes place when a vehicle exceeds the limitations of tire adhesion in a turn or a curve. It may be the result of too much steering input or approaching the corner too fast. It can also happen if you make an aggressive steering response to go around an obstacle in the road.

Third is the **power skid**. It occurs when the vehicle is pushed beyond its capacity at a given speed or for the prevalent conditions. It is the frequent result of trying to accelerate too fast, causing the tires to spin and reducing your control.

No matter what sort of skid you are in, you take the same two steps for getting out of it.

Solutions to a Skid

- **Steer in the direction of the skid.** Use rapid but smooth inputs. Anticipate a possible second skid caused by overcorrecting or a sudden regaining of traction. Straighten the wheels when you have regained control of the vehicle.

- **Cover your brakes.** In a braking skid, ease up on the brakes to the point where your wheels are no longer locked up. In a cornering or power skid, avoid using the brakes until regaining control of your vehicle.

Of course the best way to deal with a skid is to avoid it. There are a number of factors that can help you do this.

Factors in Skid Avoidance

- **Perception**—Searching at least twelve seconds ahead and maintaining an adequate following distance behind other vehicles help you avoid the need for abrupt steering and braking inputs.

- **Steering**—Proper hand positioning and steering methods minimize vehicle weight transfers.

- **Braking**—Early braking reduces the chance of having to make a sudden stop.

- **Speed control**—Excessive speed can lead to a loss of traction. The difference between skidding and not skidding may be only two to three miles per hour. Practicing speed control during normal driving helps you make better decisions during emergency responses and pursuits.

- **Roadway positioning**—The more a vehicle has to move laterally, the greater the chance that it will skid. Searching ahead may enable you to move away from a potential problem. Not being aware of your roadway position may force you to make a drastic maneuver that could cause a skid.

Review Questions

1. Why should you back into perpendicular parking spaces instead of pulling in head first?

2. What are your agency's guidelines regarding turnabouts?

3. What are the two questions that you should ask yourself before making a lane change?

4. What are the two difficult problems that you are likely to encounter when considering passing a slower vehicle on a two-lane road?

5. What should you do whenever your visibility or line of sight is restricted?

6. What steps should you take to get out of a skid?

Ten

Environmental Factors Affecting Vehicle Operations

Objectives

After completing this chapter, you will be able to

- *Identify road conditions that affect vehicle operations*
- *Understand how to read the road*
- *Understand the limitations of night driving*
- *Apply the rules for driving in bad weather*

Law enforcement officers often find themselves working in less than ideal circumstances. This includes driving on all kinds of roads in all kinds of weather. You need to understand how various environmental factors impact vehicle operations.

Road Condition

When we talk about the condition of the road, we do not just mean whether it is smooth or full of potholes. A road's condition involves a number of factors. Each of them can give you clues about what may lie ahead.

One important factor is **location**. You can learn a lot about the road by simply knowing where it is. For instance, when operating in rural areas, there is a good chance of coming upon slow moving vehicles such as tractors, farm equipment and trucks. You may also see pets, bicyclists, children waiting for school buses, and occasionally, loose livestock.

In urban areas, you should expect traffic to suddenly enter the roadway from intersections, alleys, parking lots and driveways. Drivers often exit parked cars and delivery vehicles without taking a good look around. Most important, whenever you are near parks, schools or homes, you should expect to find children playing in or near the street.

Besides location, the **type of road surface** can help you determine what to expect. Blacktop roads tend to become slick with oil bleeding to the surface on hot, humid days. During extremely hot weather, heavy traffic might cause a blacktop road to buckle into a washboard effect. This leads to extremely rough driving conditions that can affect your steering.

Concrete is heavy and settles readily. As such, it tends to have more dips and bumps than other surfaces. It has also been known to explode at joints on hot days, leading to holes in the road. During freezing conditions, concrete can glaze over very quickly, especially bridges and shaded areas.

Loose surfaces, such as dirt and gravel, frequently result in vehicles skidding around corners or sliding when braking. The tires of vehicles in front of you can often kick up stones and dust. Another problem with dirt is that it often turns to mud when wet. This can lead to the road being even more slippery, making all maneuvers that you perform more hazardous. Large build-ups of mud on tires can cause you to lose traction.

A third factor is the particular **features of the road**. The number of features you might see on a stretch of road is almost endless, with each telling you something different. For instance, dark spots often pinpoint bumps and dips. Excessive skid marks may indicate that you are approaching a hazard, such as sharp turn. A sharp turn may also be indicated by cars quickly disappearing around a curve. When the sun is low in the sky, shadows might indicate that the road is rising or falling.

Over time, you will develop a feel for the various road conditions in your area. However, no matter how much experience you have behind the wheel, there are two rules for reading the road that you should always observe. They are listed on the next page.

Rules for Reading the Road

- **Drive according to what you can see.** Whenever you are unsure about what is coming, slow down. Also reduce your speed if you cannot see over the crest of a hill, around a curve or around traffic.

- **Do not travel any faster than your ability to stop within the visible distance.** If you can only see 200 feet ahead, make sure you can stop within 200 feet. This usually gives you enough space to react safely to any obstacles in your path.

Operating a Vehicle at Night

Darkness severely limits your ability to see pedestrians, two-wheeled vehicles, stalled cars, curves and other objects. Also, judging the speed and position of other vehicles is more difficult at night. Added to that, the headlights of an approaching vehicle can further impair your visibility. All of these factors force you to make snap decisions based on sketchy and incomplete information.

The biggest problem with operating a vehicle at night is that you have to depend on your headlights. Even in the best of situations, they illuminate a short distance and only straight ahead. Sometimes this gives you very little time to react to what comes into view.

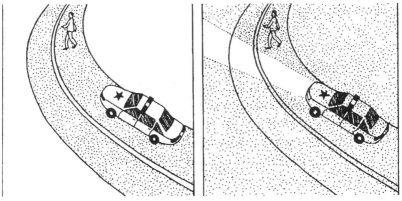

There are times, however, when you can use the limitations of your headlights to your advantage. Since light travels in a straight line, your headlights can give you some indications about the road ahead. If the roadway appears dark, it is dropping or curving. If it appears brighter as you approach an area, the road is rising.

People drive at night so frequently that it has become routine. The general public can often get away with a casual approach, but you, as a law enforcement officer, cannot. Optimally, your vehicle operations training will include night driving exercise. Whether or not you train at night, however, you must always remember to take special care when operating a vehicle after dark.

Tips for Operating a Vehicle at Night

- **Understand and acknowledge your limitations.** You must rely on your headlights at night. Darkness limits your sight, which reduces reaction times and can lead to tunnel vision. If you accept your limitations, you can make better decisions regarding speed and other nighttime maneuvers.

- **Do not overdrive your headlights.** Always drive at a speed that allows you to stop within the distance that you can see.

- **Increase your sight distance.** Keep your windshield and headlights clean. Also keep panel lights on the dashboard dim. The less light you have inside the car, the better your eyes will adjust to the limited light outside. However, you must be able to easily read the speedometer at all times.

- **Allow a greater margin of safety, especially when overtaking and passing other vehicles.** Maintain at least a four-second following distance.

- **Avoid staring at bright lights, especially headlight glare from oncoming vehicles.** The human eye takes about seven seconds to fully recover from being blinded by a bright light. At sixty miles per hour, a car travels 616 feet in seven seconds.

- **Never wear sunglasses at night.** After dark, they significantly reduce your ability to see.

Weather Conditions

Bad weather often creates an environment where it is more difficult to control your car. **Rain** can be a problem in any geographic area, at any time of the year. Even as little as 1/16th of an inch of water on the road can cause you to hydroplane, a condition where a tire rides on the water rather than the road surface. Needless to say, that will greatly affect your ability to brake and steer. Another problem is that driving through areas of water can affect brake performance and the vehicle's electrical system. If only one side of your vehicle goes through the water, the vehicle will pull in that direction.

Rain often creates another weather-related problem: **poor visibility**. A variety of other conditions can distort or blot out images, as well. Among them are smoke, haze and mist. Fog tends to collect in valleys and low-lying areas, often reducing visibility to zero. Obviously, if you cannot see, you cannot search and analyze your driving environment.

Also be alert for **windy conditions**. Wind can be difficult because it does not have to blow hard to create a problem. Even a slight breeze can lead to strong gusts as it funnels between large buildings or over hills. The danger is that a crosswind can blow a vehicle off the road or across the centerline, particularly in curves and on corners. Wet roads intensify the effects of windy conditions.

The most hazardous conditions are presented by **snow, ice and freezing rain**. Whenever they cover the roadway, your ability to stop and steer is diminished greatly. In addition, snow has a hiding effect. It can cover things such as road signs and lane marking. The edge of the road is often obscured, as well. In cold, wet weather, treacherous conditions can develop at any time. Once the temperature drops below freezing, bridges and shaded areas will ice up quickly.

Regardless of what type of bad weather you are experiencing, there are a few rules you can follow to make driving safer.

Rules for Operating a Vehicle in Bad Weather

- **Slow down but keep moving.** A reduction in speed helps keep water from building up underneath your tires and gives you more control when going around corners or through large puddles. The slower you go, the more control you have. However, you should avoid coming to a complete stop on slick roads. Once stopped, it is often hard to get going again. And when you are not moving, other vehicles have to stop or go around you. Either maneuver may result in a skid, which could lead to a collision.

- **Lengthen your following distance.** In virtually every bad weather condition, you will need more space for stopping your vehicle. Keep at least a four-second following distance to all other traffic. Watch for slow-moving or stopped vehicles. Frequently check your rear view mirror for fast-approaching vehicles.

- **Increase your visibility.** It is important that you can see and be seen. Turn on your low-beam headlights, no matter what time of day it is. This makes it easier for other motorists and pedestrians to see you. Never drive with only your parking lights on.

- **Do not make any sudden moves.** An abrupt maneuver may cause you to lose control of your vehicle. Slow down sooner than normal when approaching intersections, curves and downgrades. In addition, smooth maneuvers make you more predictable to other motorists. That may prevent them from having to react suddenly to you.

• **If conditions are very severe, pull over as far as possible and stop.** Leave your headlights on and activate your hazard lights. If you are stopped in deep snow, be aware that carbon monoxide may seep back into the vehicle if your exhaust pipe is blocked.

Review Questions

1. What are the two basic rules for reading the road?

2. What are the limitations of relying on your headlights when operating a vehicle at night?

3. What are the steps you should follow when driving at night?

4. What is hydroplaning? How can it be avoided?

5. What are the rules for driving in bad weather?

Emergency
Operations

Eleven

How an Emergency Response Affects You

Objectives

After completing this chapter, you will be able to

- *Understand the physical challenges of an emergency response*
- *Identify dangerous mental factors associated with emergency responses*
- *Apply the steps needed to control the mental aspects of operating a vehicle in an emergency mode*

Any emergency response will have a dramatic impact on you, both physically and mentally. It is important that you understand how you will be affected. If you know what to expect during an emergency response, you will be better prepared to handle the situation.

The Impact of Speed

Responding to an emergency usually requires driving at faster than normal speeds. The skills needed to do this are pretty much the same as the skills needed for non-emergency operations. But the physical requirements needed to perform these skills are heightened. To get a sense of this, consider how much more difficult it will be for you to operate within a basic system of driving.

The Effects of Increased Speed on Driving

- **Searching**—Your field of vision becomes more narrow and blurred as speed increases. Sometimes, the only clear line-of-sight is confined to the narrow area just in front of you. In effect, you develop what is known as tunnel vision.

- **Identifying**—You approach other vehicles rapidly so you have to interpret events faster. This might hinder your ability to recognize all of the factors in your driving environment. You might spot one potential hazard while failing to see another.

- **Predicting**—Your ability to forecast what other vehicles will do is reduced significantly. Many motorists overreact when they see an emergency vehicle approaching them, especially with its lights and siren on. Some motorists will brake fast; others may try an unexpected steering maneuver.

- **Deciding**—A reduced ability to search, identify and predict often results in faulty judgment and high-risk decisions.

- **Executing**—A hurried decision means a greater risk of something going wrong. In addition, higher speeds give you less margin for error in your driving maneuvers. This makes executing even the best decisions more difficult.

While safe vehicle operations is more difficult, it is still possible. Your body has an amazing ability to compensate for physical challenges. One thing in your favor is that the heightened emotions and excitement will give you a shot of adrenaline. That may increase your awareness of the situation and help you focus in on the task at hand.

However, adrenaline cannot overcome major physical obstacles. If any of your senses are not functioning properly, the process of gathering information will be further impaired. If your mind is not clear, you are less able to process data and make good decisions. If your motor skills are not up to par, the margin for error in executing your decisions is even smaller.

Your life and the lives of your fellow officers depend on you being able to respond effectively to an emergency. If you have a physical condition that reduces your effectiveness, request a different assignment until you return to normal. The risks of high-speed driving are too high. Don't take a chance. Play it safe.

The Mental Impact of Emergency Operations

The same attitudes that affect non-emergency driving also apply to emergency driving. If you have developed good attitudes, these should carry over into emergency situations. However, there are a few mental factors that tend to crop up in emergency situations.

One of the most dangerous is **aggression**. Aggressive driving leads to taking unnecessary risks. These high-risk activities usually offer low-gain results, so even success rarely justifies the chance taken. Aggressive drivers frequently operate their vehicles in a reckless manner, exposing their agencies and themselves to severe legal consequences.

Signs of Aggression

- Anger easily aroused
- Eagerness to undertake all activities in a spirit of competition
- Intense desire to win at all costs

Another common mental factor is **peer pressure**. It is fueled by pride and the fear of rejection. It is very dangerous in law enforcement because the desire to be accepted by your fellow officers may cause you to exceed your limitations. The amazing thing about peer pressure is that officers under its influence frequently take risks that they clearly know are beyond their capability. New officers in particular often feel that they must be the first unit at a scene or that they should never call off a pursuit.

Signs of Peer Pressure

- Allowing the influence of others to override your better judgment
- Believing that others have unrealistic expectations of you

A third factor is **extreme emotion**. During an emergency, you will have a mixture of emotions, such as excitement, fear, anger, anxiety and worry. These emotions can be so intense that they have a crippling effect on you. You may be so caught up in the moment that your judgment is distorted and your ability to perform necessary driving skills is reduced.

Signs of Extreme Emotion

- Immediate effects include faster heart and respiratory rates, flushed face, higher blood pressure and tense muscles
- Long-term effects include changes in appetite, digestive problems and ulcers

Overcoming the Mental Impact

The dangerous mental factors of emergency driving cannot be completely eliminated, but they can be controlled. Once you learn to do that, you increase your ability to control your vehicle and make better decisions. The end result is not only do you arrive safely at your destination, but also you arrive in control of your emotions.

Rules for Controlling the Mental Impact

- **Be assertive, not aggressive.** Being assertive is reacting strongly to the situation without going beyond the scope of your agency's policy. It is also using your driving skills to their fullest but never exceeding their limits. Assertive driving builds confidence through a knowledge that you have been trained to respond to emergency situations. That, in turn, increases your patience and good judgment.

- **Talk yourself through an emergency run.** This calms you down and gives you a better chance to accurately evaluate the situation. It may also prevent you from using your vehicle as an outlet for your hostility.

- **Never let anyone else persuade you to go against your best judgment.** Do not be afraid to back off if the situation warrants it. Ultimately, you are responsible for your actions. Make sure your actions are your own.

- **Use your emotions to your advantage.** Fear of injury coupled with the love of family and friends may keep you from exceeding your driving limits. The desire to do a good job and still be able to go home at the end of the day should point you towards high-gain, low-risk activities.

Review Questions

1. How does increased speed impact emergency vehicle operations?

2. Why is your physical condition so important when operating in an emergency mode?

3. What three mental factors are commonly associated with emergency driving? What are some of the signs of each?

4. What four steps should you take to control the mental aspects of responding to an emergency?

Twelve

Vehicle Operations during an Emergency Response

Objectives

After completing this chapter, you will be able to

- *Modify the basic skills to meet the needs of emergency operations*
- *Understand the impact of weight transfers*
- *Detail when you can and cannot cross lanes of traffic*

The skills you learn and practice for non-emergency driving will also work for emergency operations. However, due to increased speed and the influence of emotional factors, there are a few additional considerations that you should know about.

Backing

The chance for a collision is always high while moving in reverse. The chance is even higher during an emergency response. This is because officers seldom practice backing at higher speeds and with heightened emotions. For that reason, you should avoid driving in reverse unless absolutely necessary.

Of course, there will be times when you must back up to respond to an emergency. Bear in mind that while the driving situation has changed, the vehicle dynamics have not. A vehicle going backwards is extremely sensitive to driving inputs (speed, steering and braking). So no matter what situation you are in, you should follow the basic rules for driving in reverse explained in Chapter Nine. But since it is an emergency, you can add a few rules to what you already know.

Rules for Backing during an Emergency Response

- **Back in a straight line if possible.** Steering inputs have dramatic results when you are traveling at high speeds and under stress.

- **Do not rush.** Keep driving inputs smooth, normal and constant. It is better to take extra time than to hurry and possibly end up in an accident.

- **Limit backing to short distances.** If you have a lot of ground to cover, turn the vehicle around and maneuver it in a forward gear.

Controlling Speed

When it comes to the effect of increased speed, you must be concerned about **weight transfers**. Emergency operations require quick speed and space management adjustments. A sudden increase in speed causes the front end of a vehicle to lift up, transferring weight to the rear. This can result in a loss of traction in the front wheels and reduce your steering control. On the other hand, when you brake, the weight is shifted to the front. Too fast a decrease in speed may result in a skid.

With that in mind, you should remember a few things about accelerating and decelerating in an emergency.

Controlling Speed during an Emergency Response

- **All speed adjustments should be smooth.** Controlling your inputs will help you control your own emotions. Search ahead ten and twelve seconds to identify speed requirements early.

- **If you need maximum acceleration, do not stomp on the accelerator.** Use a more gradual approach. Depress the accelerator pedal 1/2 to 3/4 of the distance to the floor. This amount of pressure will ensure efficient engine and tire response. The remaining pressure can be applied based on how your vehicle is responding.

- **Avoid decelerating by changing gears on an automatic transmission.** An abrupt downshift can throw a vehicle into a skid. It can also severely damage the engine or transmission, especially if you accidentally over shift into "reverse" or "park."

Braking

Emergency braking is very similar to non-emergency braking. You will still only encounter two situations: either you have enough space and time for a controlled stop, or you have to stop your vehicle as quickly as possible.

One of the major differences between emergency and non-emergency braking is the frequency of sudden stops. It is almost a guarantee that at some time during an emergency run you will have to abruptly slow down your vehicle or bring it to a quick, sudden stop.

Tips for Braking during an Emergency Response

- **Anticipate sudden braking needs as your speed increases.** Search ten to twelve seconds ahead for potential obstacles that might create a reason for a sudden stop. Be especially alert whenever your visibility is limited.

- **Keep the brakes from overheating.** Overheated brakes may lose their ability to grab and stop wheel movement efficiently. Help keep your brakes cool by not covering the brake pedal with your left foot. Also, use your brakes sparingly. Do not keep speeding up and slowing down. If you use your brakes only when you have to, they should function properly when you need them.

Steering

During an emergency response, it is critical that you keep both hands on the steering wheel. It is easy to misjudge potential obstacles when you are traveling at higher speeds. You need the extra control the two-handed method gives you.

Higher speeds also affect a vehicle's reaction to your inputs. Adjustments that were reasonable and safe during non-emergency driving responses might get you in trouble during an emergency response. Erratic steering often leads to a need for countersteering. If you overcorrect, your vehicle can easily go into a skid.

The nine o'clock-three o'clock hand position works best in an emergency. This allows you to maneuver the steering wheel 180 degrees without breaking contact with it. The nine-three position also keeps you square and upright in the vehicle. That, too, can help you maintain control.

Tips for Steering during an Emergency Response

- **Keep all steering inputs smooth and gradual.** One thing that helps with this is identifying potential obstacles early. As before, you have a better chance of spotting a developing problem by searching ten to twelve seconds ahead.

- **Do not panic if you get into a skid.** Take your foot off the accelerator and steer in the direction that you want your vehicle to go. Be prepared for a secondary skid in the opposite direction as you come out of the first one.

100

Cornering

Increased speeds also require a higher degree of skill for negotiating turns and curves. You cannot simply be concerned with the physical characteristics of the corner. You must consider the effect of **inertia** as well. The law of inertia states that a body at rest tends to remain at rest and that a body in motion tends to remain in motion. As you turn, inertia acts as if you are still going straight. This gives your vehicle a push towards the outside edge of the lane. It also shifts the vehicle's weight to the outside, causing it to lean away from the turn.

The effect of inertia increases with speed. If you are going too fast around a corner, your tires will not be able to hold the road. This will put you into a skid. You might be able to avoid such a skid by reducing your steering input. But that may force you into another lane of traffic.

When cornering, it is critical that you **use only the available roadway**. If the lane next to you is open as you approach a corner, you may be able to swing out to give you a better angle for negotiating the turn. If it is not open, you have to stay in your own lane.

You must also be extremely cautious about crossing over into a lane of oncoming traffic. Many curves and turns have blind spots, limiting your ability to see other drivers. Just as important, it limits their ability to see you. Unless you can positively determine that there is no threat to any vehicle, you should not enter a lane of oncoming traffic.

Tips for Cornering during an Emergency Response

- **Evaluate the corner as early as possible.** If you can, search ahead ten to twelve seconds.

- **Make all lane and speed adjustments prior to reaching the corner.** If possible, position your vehicle to the outside. This will make the turn wider and allow for a faster cornering speed.

• **Select an apex based on the available roadway.** Never cut across a lane of oncoming traffic unless you are absolutely positive that it is safe to do so.

• **Once you pass through the apex, increase your speed.** You should also steer your vehicle towards the best position for exiting the corner.

Review Questions

1. What three rules should you remember about backing up during an emergency response?

2. Why are weight transfers dangerous at high speeds?

3. What technique should you use to reach your vehicle's maximum speed?

4. What is the danger of your brakes heating up? What can you do to keep them cool?

5. Why is the two-handed steering method more important in an emergency mode than in a non-emergency mode?

6. How does inertia affect your vehicle as it corners?

7. What is meant by "only use the available roadway" when cornering?

Thirteen

Using Your Equipment in an Emergency

Objectives

After completing this chapter, you will be able to

- *Use your radio effectively in an emergency*
- *Identify the emergency warning devices on your vehicle and understand their limitations*
- *Understand your state laws governing the use of emergency equipment*

Most law enforcement vehicles have equipment to help you respond rapidly to emergencies without sacrificing safety. That emergency equipment, however, does have limitations. Knowing the strengths and weaknesses of your radio and warning devices gives you the best chance for success.

Using the Radio

Because you have a functioning radio, you are never alone. By connecting you with the dispatch and other officers, your radio expands the size of the team responding to a call. It allows the coordination of activity and increases the team's effectiveness. Most important, your radio enables you to obtain assistance when you need it.

To maximize use of the radio during an emergency, you need to understand that environmental factors will impact its operation. First, some factors make your voice harder to hear. Your siren may drown out your voice completely. Other overwhelming factors include engine noise resulting from a sudden acceleration as well as the horns and loud vehicles associated with heavy traffic.

When using the radio during an emergency situation, there are a number of tips to follow. They are listed below.

Tips for Radio Use during an Emergency Response

- **Make your transmissions brief but complete.** Identify yourself and report the emergency situation. Also give your location and direction of travel.

- **Be as accurate as possible.** Inaccurate information may cause fellow officers to take the wrong actions. That can result in delays when requesting assistance.

- **Keep your voice calm, natural and relaxed.** Speak loud enough to be heard clearly but try not to get too excited. If you are too excited, your transmissions may not be understood by the dispatch and other units.

- **Be efficient and safe.** If two officers are assigned to your vehicle, the person who is not driving should handle radio communications. If you are in a single assignment unit, exercise great caution. Using the radio while driving at increased speeds is very dangerous. Speak only when it is safe to do so. Do not let others dictate how you use the radio.

Emergency Warning Devices

You can never accurately predict how motorists and pedestrians will react to an approaching law enforcement vehicle. However, when sufficiently notified, they have a better chance of responding in a safe manner. For this reason, sirens and emergency lights are usually required by legal statutes for all emergency responses, regardless of your location or the time of day.

While warning devices are effective, there are a number of factors that affect their use. First, **weather conditions** have a significant impact. On clear days, your lights may be seen from a great distance, but your siren tends to fade into the atmosphere. However, when it is overcast or cloudy, your siren can be heard at longer distances, but the effect of your lights may be diminished.

If there is fog in the area, the moisture in the air will carry sound with a minimum loss of decibels for a short distance. But as the distance increases, there will be significant sound blockage. Your emergency lights may be ineffective in foggy weather. Inclement weather, such as heavy rain or snow, greatly reduces the value of both the siren and lights. The quality of your driving then becomes even more critical.

Location is another factor that affects your emergency devices. The siren may be less noticeable in a residential area. Large trees and hedges tend to absorb sound. In commercial areas, tall buildings can block vision and deflect sound. Pedestrians and other motorists may not notice you until you are right on top of them. Siren and lights are most effective in flat, open areas.

A third factor is **traffic conditions**. Sirens become less discernible with the increase of traffic noise. Loud vehicles, such as heavy trucks and buses, can completely drown out a siren. Large trucks and vans may block the view of your emergency lights to other drivers. Great care and caution must be taken in areas congested with foot traffic, especially school zones and parks.

Bear in mind that your **emergency warning devices are not substitutes for caution and good driving skills.** Other drivers are not always attentive. They may be distracted by such things as their own radios, children misbehaving, telephone conversations, and conversations with other passengers. The effects of these distractions are heightened if the windows are rolled up or if the fan is running. Even without multiple distractions, the vast majority of drivers with their windows up cannot tell from which direction a siren is coming.

Speed has a dramatic impact, too. **As your speed goes up, the effectiveness of your equipment goes down.** Due to an increase in the feet traveled per second by your vehicle, other people have less time to react to your approach. A driver in front of you may not notice you until you are only one or two car lengths away.

Another problem might be due to other law enforcement activity in an area. It might be another unit responding to the same situation as you or possibly another situation altogether. Whichever it is, a person may notice one set of emergency warning devices but not another.

As you can see, even under ideal conditions, you can easily surprise another motorist or a pedestrian. People, when surprised, tend to have erratic responses. That can lead to panic stopping, panic steering or sudden acceleration.

There are several things you can do to make your emergency lights and siren more effective. They are listed below.

Tips for Using Your Emergency Warning Devices

- **Use your headlights.** In the daytime, your high beams are easier to see than traditional red or blue overhead lights. Emergency flashers help as well. But do not use high beams after dark. They can obliterate the emergency lights and blind oncoming traffic.

- **Change your siren patterns.** The alternating sounds will draw more attention.

- **Slow down when near pedestrians, especially in school zones.** This gives people more time to notice your approach and respond safely.

- **Expect the unexpected.** Even with ample warning about your approach, the reactions of pedestrians and other motorists are unpredictable.

Your emergency warning devices can also have an adverse effect on you. A siren often drowns out the sounds associated with going fast, such as wind and engine noise. This might cause you to misjudge your speed and distort your perception of what is happening around you.

Above all, **beware of the "Invincibility Syndrome."** The use of emergency lights and siren often give a false sense of security. Just because you are using your warning devices does not mean that the general public will respond to your approach. Your lights and siren are nothing more than tools of communication. The responsibility of safe operations still rests with you.

Review Questions

1. Why is your radio your most important piece of equipment?

2. List the four steps for effective radio communication.

3. What emergency warning devices are required by your state statutes for an emergency response?

4. What effect does vehicle speed have on your siren?

5. What is the "Invincibility Syndrome?"

6. What are the four steps you can take to increase the effectiveness of your emergency warning devices?

Fourteen

Route Selection

Objectives

After completing this chapter, you will be able to

- *Identify the factors that affect route selection during an emergency response*
- *Use a checklist for route selection*
- *Practice selecting the best routes*

When responding to an emergency, you need to reach your destination as fast as possible. However, the amount of time it takes to get there is a secondary issue. The most important consideration is safety. It is possible to respond quickly and safely to an emergency call. Selecting the best route of travel is a crucial part of that goal.

Factors Affecting Route Selection

There are a number of **factors to consider when selecting a route.** First is traffic density. Avoid roads with heavy or difficult-to-navigate traffic patterns. These areas include commercial zones, construction sites, special entertainment events and areas prone to bumper-to-bumper traffic. Avoid roads that serve large or slow moving vehicles such as tractor trailers and farm equipment.

Also consider **pedestrian traffic.** Stay away from areas such as school zones, parks and other places where children may be playing. Also avoid busy intersections and bus stops.

Line-of-sight restrictions is another factor. Select a route that offers good visibility, both for you and the general public. Avoid roads that have a significant number of hills, curves or parked vehicles along the side. Wide-open intersections offer the best visibility for everybody. One-way streets offer you the advantage of not having to deal with oncoming traffic, but they do force you to approach all other vehicles from the rear. That is the area other drivers tend to be least aware of.

Another consideration is **road conditions**. Non-paved roads tend to offer less traction. This can become a serious issue at higher speeds, especially on curves. Also areas with rough pavement, potholes and bumps limit your control and force you to slow down.

Weather conditions play an important role. During bad weather, select routes that are best equipped to handle poor driving conditions. For instance, when it is raining, choose a route that has good drainage capabilities. During a snow or ice storm, use the main thoroughfares. They are the streets that are usually cleared first.

The last factors to consider are **time of day** and **day of the week**. A commercial zone may be packed with traffic during normal business hours, especially in the early morning and late afternoon. However, the same area may seem deserted at night and on the weekends.

Processing all of the factors needed to make a choice can be difficult. To help do this, there are a few questions you that should ask yourself when choosing a route. They can serve as a route-selection checklist.

Checklist for Route Selection

- Is this route the quickest and most direct?
- Do the intersections along the way offer acceptable lines-of-sight and legal rights-of-way?
- Does the route have the fewest number of obstacles that can inhibit people from seeing or hearing my emergency warning devices?

- Does the route require the least number of steering and speed adjustments?
- Are the thoroughfares wide, and do they have numerous escape options for avoiding collisions?

Practicing Route Selection

Most officers rarely consider route selection because it is a low priority in non-emergency response. But then when an emergency situation comes up, they are not equipped to choose a route with confidence and authority.

You can avoid that predicament by practicing route selection. When responding to a non-emergency call, choose your route as if it were an emergency. Think about your trip there after arriving at your destination and ask yourself if the route taken was the best one available. If it wasn't, consider why not and what route might have been a better choice. By routinely analyzing your actions, you develop the confidence and skill to select the best route when it really matters.

Review Questions

1. What are some of the factors that influence route selection?

2. What five questions should serve as a checklist for route selection?

3. How can you practice route selection?

Fifteen

Collisions

Objectives

After completing this chapter, you will be able to

- *Describe the three impacts that can occur in a collision*
- *Explain what "good space management" means*
- *Detail the steps for clearing an intersection*
- *Explain when to take evasive steering and detail the steps for doing so*
- *Explain what to do if you cannot avoid a collision*

Collisions happen all too frequently, especially during emergency situations. The excitement and urgency of a critical response can distract your driving efforts. And you cannot predict how the public will react to your emergency warning devices. Anything can happen; you have to be prepared.

The Three Impacts

If you were in a collision, you could be subjected to three separate impacts. The first is the **vehicle impact**. As the name implies, it occurs when your vehicle strikes a fixed object or another vehicle. When that happens, your vehicle can come to a complete stop in less than one second.

Second is the **human impact**. While your vehicle is coming to a stop, you will continue moving at the collision speed until something makes you stop. If you are not restrained by a safety belt, you will probably hit the steering wheel or windshield. The force of this impact can be devastating. For instance, if you hit the windshield as the result of collision while driving forty miles per hour, the force of the blow would be same as if you fell off of a five-story building or drove off a fifty-foot cliff.

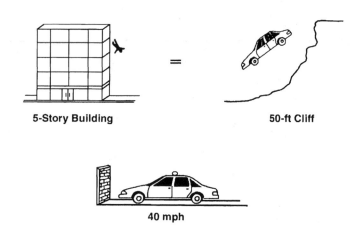

5-Story Building   **50-ft Cliff**

40 mph

Last is the **internal impact**. This takes place inside your body when your brain slams against your skull or internal organs hit the skeletal frame. Internal injuries frequently kill a crash victim, but they are not always immediately detectable. Death can occur days later.

Avoiding Collisions

Obviously, the best way to avoid the three impacts is to avoid being in a traffic accident. You can help prevent collisions with good **space management**. The goal of space management is to control your path of travel by maintaining a safety cushion around your vehicle. You establish this cushion by adjusting your following distance of other vehicles to meet existing traffic conditions. This cushion also prevents you from being boxed in on the sides and to the rear.

Once the cushion is established, you should continually scan ahead of your vehicle, both far and near. This enables you to spot potential obstacles and make corrections to your path of travel. Searching ahead also allows you to analyze possible avenues of escape.

Take special care to **clear intersections** before entering them. Driving through an intersection during an emergency response is one of the most dangerous things that you will ever do. Many officers have been injured and killed performing that maneuver. And since intersections are where most third-party collisions occur, it should be no surprise that this is the most highly litigated area of law enforcement vehicle operations.

Even though your emergency lights and siren allow you to disregard many traffic laws, you are still obligated to drive in a responsible, safe manner. Taking prudent steps before entering an intersection will help protect the general public and you.

Tips for Clearing Intersections

- **Come to a stop before entering the intersection. At a minimum, be prepared to stop.** Just because your lights and siren are on does not mean that all traffic will give you the right-of-way. If pedestrians and other vehicles do not stop, you must yield.

- **Identify potential obstacles by using quick searching methods.** Do not blindly go through any intersection. Cars and trucks may be stopped, but that does not guarantee they have noticed you.

- **Attract as much attention as you can.** Change siren patterns to avoid giving off one set of sounds. Adjust your speed to give people time to react safely.

- **Look for other emergency vehicles.** Your siren may prevent you from hearing them. At the same time, their sirens may prevent them from hearing you.

115

Even when you exercise great caution, you may find your path blocked suddenly and without warning. Should that happen, use **evasive steering**. Evasive steering is an abrupt change of your path of travel. To accomplish this safely, you need plenty of room to move from side to side or lane to lane.

Steps for Evasive Steering

1. Position your hands at the nine o'clock-three o'clock steering location on the steering wheel.

2. Turn the steering wheel no more than 1/2 rotation in the direction you want to go.

3. Turn the wheel back in the opposite direction to correct for the initial swerve.

4. Return the wheel to the straight-ahead position. Additional movements of the wheel may be necessary to keep the back end from swaying.

If you cannot swerve to avoid a collision, your only other option is **sudden braking**. If you are lucky, you will have enough distance to stop safely. However, there are occasions when a collision may be unavoidable.

Being Involved in a Collision

Just because you are about to hit an object does not mean that you have no control over the incident. Take steps to reduce your chance of injury and minimize the damage to your vehicle.

What to Do if a Collision Is Inevitable

• **Try to strike the object at an angle.** This deflects some of the impact force. Head-on collisions absorb the entire impact.

- **Avoid having the collision take place in the driver's quarter of the vehicle.** The point of impact should be as far away from you as possible.

- **Maintain steering and braking control.** This might enable you to avoid colliding with additional objects after the first collision. The incident is not over until all of the vehicles involved have come to a complete stop. Until then, you have to be ready to react to whatever happens.

The most important thing you can do is **wear your safety belt at all times.** If you are restrained in your seat, you will stop as your vehicle stops. This is known as **riding down the collision.** It reduces the severity of the human and internal impacts and can save your life. In addition, a safety belt helps you maintain your position inside the vehicle, giving you a better chance to keep control of the car and avoid secondary collisions.

Review Questions

1. What are the three types of impacts that can occur in a collision?

2. What is your agency's practice on coming to a complete stop before entering an intersection?

3. What are the best ways to avoid a collision? When should you use each one of them?

4. What does "riding down the collision" mean?

Pursuits

Sixteen

The Foundation of Pursuits

Objectives

After completing this chapter, you will be able to

- *Define what a pursuit is*
- *Explain how pursuit operations are different from other forms of emergency vehicle operations*

Over the course of your career, you will probably face a number of potentially lethal situations. When most officers think about that, they picture a confrontation with an armed, combatant felon. However, statistics show that you will use your weapon very few times as compared to the number of times that you will be involved in a pursuit.

What Is a Pursuit?

It is difficult to determine the exact number of pursuits that take place each year. One reason is that not all agencies define a pursuit in the same way. Another reason is that not all pursuits are reported. Frequently, we find out about an incident only if a collision takes place. Then the pursuit is listed because of the need to file an accident report. Even though the statistics are inaccurate, we do know that pursuits happen every day.

As defined for this book, **a pursuit is an attempt by a peace officer in an emergency vehicle to apprehend a person in another motor vehicle who is willfully failing to stop**. The key is that a suspect is "willfully failing to stop." Following a person who has not seen your signals to stop is not a pursuit. Should that person see you and still refuse to stop, you have a decision to make. If you decide to attempt an apprehension by engaging your emergency lights and siren in accordance with your state statute, then you are in a pursuit mode.

Pursuits are extremely dangerous. Most fleeing suspects are only concerned with avoiding apprehension. They might lead you into dangerous situations, hoping you lose control of your vehicle or collide with another car. The dangers are heightened by the fact that officers tend to become emotionally involved. If this happens to you, you might expose yourself to risks that you would not normally take. Far too often, the end result is injury or death, frequently to innocent third parties. The terrible consequences are compounded by lawsuits against officers, agencies and municipalities that can result in judgments in the millions of dollars.

Given the outcomes, many communities debate whether pursuits are worth the risks. People in some locations question whether pursuits should be banned altogether. However, that may cause more problems than it solves.

Problems Potentially Created by Banning Pursuits

- **You will have a credibility problem.** Violators will know that you have limited means at your disposal for making apprehensions.

- **The dangers to the public might increase.** Suspects will understand that all they have to do to get away from you is run a red light at a high rate of speed or drive in some other reckless fashion.

Despite all of the risks, most citizens support their peace officers. The public still wants and expects its law enforcement agencies to pursue fleeing suspects. However, the collective wish seems to be that an officer should initiate a pursuit only when it is absolutely necessary.

How Pursuit Operations Are Different

There are a number of ways in which pursuit operations are different from other modes of emergency vehicle operations. First, you are forced to make many more critical decisions. For a typical emergency situation, the central dispatch communicates a need for a response. If you are available, you drive to the scene without giving much thought about whether you should respond. In a pursuit, however, you must first decide whether the pursuit should be initiated. Then you must analyze ever-changing conditions and decide whether you should continue the pursuit. If you opt to terminate, you have to determine the best way to do so. All of these judgments must be made knowing that a bad decision can be disastrous.

Second, you have little control over the situation. The fleeing suspect generally dictates the speed and path of travel. And since most suspects have little or no regard for safety, you will find yourself facing a number of factors that could be avoided in a typical emergency response situation. These include factors such as vehicle positioning, speed progression and tunnel vision. They and other common pitfalls are discussed in the chapter on Pursuit Tactics.

Third, there are more participants in a pursuit than in other forms of vehicle operations. Obviously, one of the other participants is the fleeing suspect. But there might be additional participants on your team, such as the dispatch or a supervisor.

The dispatch has a number of important tasks in a pursuit. Some of them are listed below.

Role of a Dispatch in a Pursuit

- Document the initial information about the pursuit.
- Notify a supervisor, if one is available.
- Clear the radio and give you priority status.
- Begin vehicle and identification checks of the fleeing suspect and get that information radioed to you if identification can be made.

- Arrange for backup units and assistance.
- Notify any neighboring jurisdiction where a pursuit may encroach on an adjoining territory.

A supervisor also plays a critical function. However, many agencies do not have supervisors available for pursuits. If your agency does not task supervisors with pursuit oversight or if a supervisor is not available, these decisions and responsibilities may be yours.

Role of a Supervisor in a Pursuit

- Monitor and control the pursuit, directing all ground and air units involved.
- Approve and coordinate tactics, especially if deadly force becomes necessary.
- Approve or disapprove the leaving of the normal jurisdiction of the department to continue the pursuit in another department's jurisdiction.
- Have the final say in the decision to initiate, continue or terminate a pursuit.
- Conduct a post-pursuit incident review and analysis.

The Importance of a Pursuit Policy

Like other uses of lethal force, pursuits should be governed by policy. In the past, many policies were based on a concept known as **custom of usage**. This is where the policies were not specific and allowed a broad interpretation. The officers had the leeway to handle pursuits in any way they saw fit. The only requirement was that they use their best judgment. As the number of lawsuits increased over time and the cost of judgments skyrocketed, it became increasingly clear that policies based on custom of usage were not adequate.

Today, pursuit policies tend to be more restrictive. They provide carefully defined restraints, allowing for close supervision and review. This helps maintain the basic law enforcement mission to protect and serve the public while minimizing the risk of injuries and deaths. Never forget that the guidelines set forth by state law and agency policy are not optional. You are bound by these restrictions whether you agree with them or not. You must be absolutely sure what your state law and agency policy allow you to do. Just as important, you must be absolutely sure what they prohibit you from doing. And you must never, ever exceed those limitations.

While a restrictive policy does limit your actions, you should not consider it a hindrance. Actually, a restrictive policy provides several benefits for you.

Advantages of a Restrictive Policy

- **Shows what is expected of you.** Throughout the process of accomplishing a specific mission, your role and responsibility are clearly defined. This promotes consistency and professionalism.

- **Protects you from unnecessary danger.** The policy is designed to help you do your job while taking into account your own safety. It also takes into account the safety of the general public and the suspect who is fleeing from you.

- **Reduces the risk of liability proceedings.** By outlining the methods of operation, the policy shows you what your limits are. As long as you do not exceed those limits, the chances of being held liable for an injury or death are minimized.

A policy must be based on street reality. One that does not address "real world" situations serves no purpose. You will not be able to do your job, and society will not get the protection and service that it wants and demands. If you find that your policy is inadequate, inform your supervisor and management of the problem.

Of course, no matter how good a policy is, it will not be effective if you do not clearly understand it. You have to do more than just read it; you have to apply it to your everyday job tasks. Review your policy regularly to strengthen your grasp of it. The policy worksheet in the appendix to this book can help.

Another policy exercise involves your television. It seems that nearly every night there is some show that presents video clips of actual pursuits. Whenever you see one of these, think of how your policy would govern a similar incident and what you would do if you were in that situation. Those shows are good opportunities to reinforce the details of your pursuit policy and to learn from other officers' experiences.

The importance of your agency's pursuit policy cannot be overemphasized. Your policy frames the questions that you must ask yourself before taking action. It also frames the questions that will be used to review your actions after the incident is over. If you do not fully understand the directives that govern a pursuit, you should not engage in pursuit activity.

Review Questions

1. How does your agency define "pursuit?"

2. How are pursuit operations different from other modes of law enforcement driving?

3. What is meant by a policy being based on custom of usage? How is that dangerous for you?

4. What are the advantages of being under a restrictive pursuit policy?

Seventeen

Initiating a Pursuit

Objectives

After completing this chapter, you will be able to

- *Apply the test of reasonableness to your actions*
- *List the factors that need to be considered in a pursuit decision*
- *Understand what information needs to be transmitted to the dispatch if you decide to initiate a pursuit*
- *Explain the steps to take if you decide not to pursue a suspect*

Most officers believe that the majority of pursuits involve the apprehension of serious criminals. However, this is not true. The vast majority of pursuits are initiated because of misdemeanor traffic violations. Deciding when to initiate a pursuit is a difficult task. This chapter will help you make the proper decision.

The Test of Reasonableness

When it comes to pursuits, safety must take precedence over all other considerations. With that in mind, a decision to pursue has to meet **the test of reasonableness**. You need to conduct this test before you begin a pursuit because it will be used to review your actions after the incident is over. You will be judged by juries and individuals from the average person's point of view. They are the ones who see you as the protector of lives and property. They are the ones who demand high ethical conduct on your part. They will be the ones who have to be convinced that you acted properly. So before each and every pursuit, you have to ask yourself a crucial question:

Question to Be Used as a Test of Reasonableness

"If I initiate this pursuit and it results in an injury, death or property damage, would a reasonable person find that my actions were justified?"

The best way to ensure your actions meet this test is to base your pursuit decision on what you know, not what you feel. If you are like most officers, you will consider a fleeing suspect to be a personal challenge. That feeling is normal, but it must not be a factor in your decision. The simple fact that someone is fleeing is not a justifiable reason for initiating a high-speed pursuit.

Before engaging in a pursuit, you must totally understand your role. By and large the general public views you as a protector of lives and property. You must recognize that your duty as a protector of society extends not just to the general public, but to yourself, your fellow officers and even the fleeing suspect. It is imperative that you maintain the highest ethical and professional standards during all aspects of a pursuit.

You must remain focused on the task at hand and the skills required to complete that task. You cannot allow yourself to become emotionally or personally involved. While suspects cannot be allowed to freely use the roadways for unlawful purposes, law enforcement officers cannot engage in pursuits with reckless disregard for the safety of the general public.

Factors to Consider in a Pursuit Decision

- **Do you know what you are authorized to do?** The guidelines set forth by state law and your agency's policy are not optional. Under no circumstances can you exceed those restrictions. If you do not have a clear understanding of what state law and agency policy allows for your particular circumstance, then you must not initiate the pursuit.

- **How dangerous is the suspect?** There should be a probable risk that the suspect will cause an injury or death if allowed to flee. You can determine the risk posed by a suspect two ways. First, you might have suspicions that the suspect has committed a dangerous felony offense. Second, you might observe the suspect acting in a manner that poses an immediate threat to the public, such as driving recklessly. Your state statute and agency policy can provide more details on the types of offenses that constitute an immediate threat.

- **Is there a need for immediate apprehension?** If you can identify the suspect, you may be able to safely and efficiently apprehend him at a later time. However, even a positive identification cannot overcome a clear and present danger to the public. If the risk of letting him go is too high, you should attempt to apprehend him now.

- **Are you mentally and physically capable of conducting a pursuit?** A pursuit can be very stressful. That stress may affect your ability to weigh the situation objectively and make proper decisions. You must be able to control your emotions, remain calm and stay focused. In addition, you must take into account your personal condition. If you are fatigued or do not have a clear mind for some reason, you may not be able to cope safely with the physical demands of a pursuit. If you have any doubts about your mental or physical state, do not initiate. The risk is just too high.

- **Is your vehicle equipped to handle a pursuit?** Your vehicle must meet all requirements of your state statutes and agency policy for emergency vehicle operations. Anything short of full compliance might strip you of protection from liability proceedings should something go wrong. You must also have confidence that your vehicle will be able to respond to the demands you place on it. You especially need good tires and brakes. If there are any mechanical problems, you should not engage.

- **Do environmental conditions favor a successful outcome?** The actual speed of the fleeing vehicle will likely be controlled by traffic conditions, which will continually change and will require ongoing evaluation on your part. Take into account the area you are in and your familiarity with it. Also consider the time of day, the weather, roadway conditions and any other factor that could impact a high-speed chase. If visibility is limited or if you are likely to encounter pedestrians (especially children), then the risk to the public will probably outweigh the benefits of apprehending the suspect.

It is important that you understand you need to consider these factors even if your agency policy requires that a supervisor authorize all pursuits. The only facts used by a supervisor to make a decision are the facts that you supply. So even if the decision is made for you, you have to understand what your policy requires. If you do not, you will not know what information you must give.

Making a Decision

When making a pursuit decision, you must be very selective. All factors must point to "go." If you do decide to pursue, you should immediately notify the dispatch of your decision, giving the information listed below. It is good idea to communicate this information prior to turning on your emergency lights and siren. In many cases, the activation of lights and siren is what turns a traffic stop into a pursuit situation. Communicating this information before the suspect flees allows you to concentrate on safe driving techniques as the suspect tries to elude you.

Information to Be Communicated to the Dispatch

- **Identify yourself.** Give your vehicle unit number, exact location, speed and direction of travel.

- **Give a description of the fleeing vehicle.** Bits of information such as the make, model, color and license plate number can be used to identify the suspect. Also indicate the number of occupants in the vehicle and give a description of each. If identification can be made, you may be able to call off the pursuit and apprehend the suspect at a later time.

- **Outline your reasons for initiating the pursuit.** This serves two purposes. First, giving clear, concise reasons begins to build the record of what happened in a particular incident. Second, transmitting your thoughts brings other people into the pursuit. You are still responsible for your actions, but if your reasons for acting are faulty, someone may catch it and convince you to disengage before a tragedy occurs.

Of course, it is possible that the best decision is not to pursue a fleeing suspect. A failure to pursue is not a reflection of your courage or desire to perform your duty. On the contrary, it may be evidence that you are performing your duty at the highest level. As stated earlier, your first obligation is to the

131

public that you have sworn to protect. If a pursuit would cause you to ignore that obligation, you must not engage. At all times, the safety of all must be your overriding concern.

Deciding not to pursue is not the same as giving up or letting him get away. You can still take action.

What to Do if You Decide Not to Pursue

- **Try to identify the suspect.** Give the dispatch the same data that you would give if you decided to pursue. Concentrate on the specific information that may be used to identify the suspect.

- **Detail your reasons for not pursuing the suspect.** Since your primary obligation is to protect the public, you should focus on safety concerns.

Review Questions

1. What is the test of reasonableness? How does it apply to a decision to initiate a pursuit?

2. According to your agency's policy, when would you be authorized to initiate a pursuit?

3. What factors should you consider when making a decision whether to pursue a fleeing suspect?

4. What information should be communicated to the dispatch if you decide to pursue a suspect?

5. What should you do if you decide not to pursue a suspect?

Eighteen

Pursuit Tactics

Objectives

After completing this chapter, you will be able to

- *Apply a test of reasonableness for continued action*
- *List the safety considerations relating to pursuits*
- *Avoid some of the common pitfalls of pursuing*
- *Explain the roles of a backup and assisting units*
- *Understand your agency's policy on pursuing within allied jurisdictions*

Once you make the decision to initiate a pursuit, your actions must be second nature. You must be able to act in accordance with state statutes and your agency's policy. This chapter helps you do that by discussing what you are likely to encounter.

Fleeing Suspects

Fleeing suspects experience the same stress as the officers who pursue them. However, the effects of that stress are much different. While officers must maintain control of their emotions and attitudes, fleeing suspects do not. Suspects do not need to remain calm and often believe they have much to gain by taking unnecessary risks. Physical factors such as fatigue, poor physical fitness and impairment (often from drugs and alcohol) can impact their psychological state. Fleeing suspects have little or no regard for their own safety, much less the safety of others. As such, they often use a number of tactics.

Possible Tactics Used by Fleeing Suspects

- Drive as fast as possible in an attempt to simply outrun a pursuing officer.
- Accelerate to a high speed, lose sight of the officer and stop. This may give the suspects the chance to change positions within a vehicle, hide the vehicle itself, or flee on foot.
- Time or delay driving maneuvers in an attempt to cause a third party to inhibit or collide with a pursuing officer.
- Violate motor vehicle laws to increase their advantage over a pursuing officer. This might include ignoring traffic controls, driving off roadways, cutting across private property and driving on the wrong side of the road or the wrong way on one-way streets.
- Use vehicle as a weapon against a pursuing officer.

A Continuous Test of Reasonableness

The danger of a pursuit cannot be overstated. At best, a pursuit involves several speeding vehicles on a roadway shared with unsuspecting motorists who could be easily injured or killed. Given that **safety must always take precedence over everything else**, you have to continually apply the test of reasonableness. At all times, the benefit of the apprehension must outweigh the risk of the pursuit itself. The problem is that the situation changes frequently and rapidly. Each change requires a reaction on your part for which you will be held accountable. So you must constantly ask yourself the following question:

Question to Ask while Pursuing

"Based on how the situation has changed, if this pursuit results in injury, death or property damage, would a reasonable person find that my actions were justified?"

Do not wait for a reason to terminate. Instead, always look for a reason to continue. As just stated, your first objective is maintaining the safety of everybody involved, which includes the general public, your fellow officers, you, and even the fleeing suspect. **You must call off the pursuit whenever you no longer have a clear, compelling reason for continuing.** To go on without one would be judged as unreasonable and would place undue risk on the safety of others.

Pursuit Procedures

When you are in a pursuit mode, you have very little control of the situation. The fleeing suspect will determine the route taken and the speed. All you can do is react and try to influence his decisions. While you are doing that, you are still obligated to drive with due regard for your safety and the safety of others, including that of the fleeing suspect.

Safety Considerations when Pursuing

- **Always leave yourself an out.** Try to maintain a space cushion around your vehicle. Your following distance should increase as speeds increase. **A gap of approximately four seconds should allow you to maintain contact safely.** In addition, never pass the suspect vehicle and do not pull up along side it unless you are executing an authorized "use of force" pursuit tactic. Both of those maneuvers will expose you to excessive risk.

- **Do not attempt to apply psychological pressure on the suspect.** The most common mistake is to close the distance on the suspect to try to convince him to stop. There is no substantial advantage to this tactic as it exposes the suspect, the public and you to unnecessary danger. It may even increase the danger by making the suspect more desperate.

- **Only go as fast as you have to.** If you exceed your limitations, you will be demonstrating willful disregard for the lives and property of others. That could subject you to liability.

- **Maintain optimum line-of-sight conditions.** Drive near the center line of the roadway whenever possible. This will give you the best lines of sight and will increase your visibility to other motorists.

- **Come to a stop before entering an intersection. At a minimum, be prepared to stop.** This is where the vast majority of collisions occur. Other motorists may not see or hear you as you approach.

- **Assist any injured third party.** If a pedestrian or another motorist is injured, disengage from the pursuit to provide aid. Other officers may be able to engage in the pursuit after you have terminated.

It is also important that you **maintain good communication** with both the general public and your fellow officers. One way you maintain communication with the general public is through vehicle positioning. You must continually adjust your position in relation to traffic on the roadway. This gives other motorists the best chance to see you as you approach. You also communicate with the public by use of emergency lights and sirens. However, be aware that your lights and siren do have limitations. These are discussed in more detail later in this chapter.

Good communication with your fellow officers requires a team approach. This enables you to get assistance when you need it and helps eliminate possible avenues of escape for the fleeing suspect. You have to keep your supervisor, central dispatch and backup units updated on your location, speed and direction of travel. Also include any additional factors that might help with the identification of the suspect as well as your reasons for continuing the chase. At some point, you may have to make a case for using some level of force to terminate the pursuit.

Tips for Maintaining Good Radio Communication

- **Reduce environmental distractions.** Turn up the volume of your radio and keep the windows closed or only slightly open.

- **Be precise.** Brevity and conciseness are the keys to good communication. Inaccurate information may cause other officers to take inappropriate actions and can result in a delayed assistance. Focus on what needs to be said.

- **Control your emotions.** Concentrate on voice quality. A calm voice is easier to understand than an excited one. Taking several deep breaths before transmitting helps control the rate of speech.

- **Anticipate the route and the suspect's moves.** Officers involved in pursuits have a tendency to broadcast where they have been instead of where they are going. Cross streets should be announced as you approach them. Identify the lane positioning of the suspect. That can be a clue as to the suspect's intended action.

- **Delegate broadcast responsibilities.** If a partner is riding with you, he or she should handle the radio while you concentrate on driving.

- **Communicate when and where the suspect's vehicle stops.** Assisting officers must know your exact location if you need help in establishing control. Also, a pursuit does not always end when the other car stops. If the suspect attempts to flee on foot, assisting officers need to know where the foot pursuit started and the direction the suspect headed.

As important as radio communication is, it cannot supersede the importance of safe vehicle operations. As stated earlier, safety must take precedence over everything else.

Common Pitfalls of Pursuing

Whenever you are pursuing a fleeing suspect, there are a few common dangers to which many officers fall prey. The most dangerous is **making the pursuit a personal challenge**. Since a pursuit is an emergency response, psychological pressures such as high emotions, social image, ego, stress and peer pressure can cloud your judgment. This might cause you to momentarily forget your agency's policy. In extreme cases, emotional involvement has led some officers to willfully ignore policy. There are documented cases where officers failed to call in a pursuit for fear of being directed to stop. There are also cases of officers misrepresenting the facts so that they would be allowed to continue the chase. It does not matter if you forget the policy or ignore it, the end result will be the same: You will be held directly responsible for your actions.

Not Letting a Pursuit Become a Personal Challenge

- **Be prepared to change your objective.** If the suspect will not stop, do not become more determined to force the issue. Instead, change your objective to identifying him. A positive identification might enable you to apprehend the suspect safely and efficiently at another time.

- **Get more people involved.** If the confrontation is only between you and the suspect, you are more likely to view it as a competition. But if you stay in constant communication with your supervisor, dispatch and other units, the confrontation involves many different people. That helps keep you focused on operating as a contributing member of a professional team.

Another risk is **duplicating the driving maneuvers of the suspect**. In the heat of the moment, officers can develop tunnel vision and begin mimicking the suspect. This is extremely dangerous because as mentioned before, a fleeing suspect often has little or no regard for safety. In an attempt to avoid apprehension, he may use his vehicle as a weapon. He may also try to force you into a collision by driving in the wrong lane, driving off the roadway, speeding through intersections, or performing any of a number of other dangerous actions.

There are occasions, however, when you might be able to duplicate the maneuvers of a suspect. An example could be taking a shortcut across a vacant parking lot or using the whole roadway whenever traffic conditions permit. Whenever doing this, you must use extreme caution. And of course, all maneuvers must conform to your agency's pursuit policy.

As you follow a suspect, be aware of the phenomenon known as **speed progression**. This is where the speed of the vehicles involved seems to increase on an ongoing basis. As you maintain contact with the suspect, he may increase his speed to try to outrun you. You then have to increase your speed to maintain contact, which in turn, leads the suspect to further increase his speed. You must avoid reaching the point where your efforts to keep up with the suspect results in you making a decision to take unreasonable actions. Whenever you are in a pursuit mode, you should strive to sustain the pursuit without losing control of the situation.

A third pitfall is **giving in to the "Invincibility Syndrome."** This was discussed in the section on Emergency Operations, but it is so important that it must be mentioned again. Many officers think that all other traffic will yield to them because of their emergency lights and siren. These devices are not substitutes for caution and utilization of professional skills. They have limitations. And they do not relieve you of your obligation to exercise due care for the safety of others.

Limitations of Emergency Warning Devices

- **You can easily outrun your siren.** When you are travelling at approximately sixty miles per hour, other people will begin hearing your siren at almost the same time you reach them. This dramatically cuts down their ability to react safely.

- **The suspect's vehicle has no emergency equipment.** Other motorists might be able to safely prepare for your approach, but they will have little or no time to avoid the suspect, who has no warning devices.

- **Environmental conditions can reduce the effectiveness of lights and sirens.** Lights may be hard to see in inclement weather. Sirens can dissipate on clear days. Heavy traffic may make lights difficult to see and sirens hard to hear. Buildings can block or deflect sound. Things in cars such as telephones, stereos, misbehaving children and air conditioners can mask an approaching siren.

- **The reaction of the general public is unpredictable.** The vast majority of motorists driving with their windows up cannot tell from which direction a siren is coming. This often leads to drivers being startled. Responses might be panic stops, panic steering or sudden acceleration.

Being a Backup Unit

Most agencies have a maximum number of units that can be involved in pursuit. Frequently, this number is one or two, meaning one lead vehicle and at most, one backup. The goal is to avoid long caravans of emergency vehicles chasing a suspect. A large number of cars will not make the pursuit more effective and will increase the danger to the general public.

You must know what your policy says about secondary units and their roles in a pursuit. Most policies state that you should not join a pursuit as a backup unit unless requested to do so by the primary unit or a supervisor. There are times, however, when the decision to pursue as a backup might be yours. This could happen if you are with the primary unit when the pursuit starts and the lead officer does not have time to make a request for assistance.

Role of a Backup in a Pursuit

- **Assist in any way possible.** The primary unit officer or a supervisor is in charge. Be ready to do whatever they ask. Of course, as you assist, always maintain a safe following distance behind the primary unit and suspect.

- **Be prepared to take over as the primary unit.** Should the first vehicle become disabled for some reason, you may have to assume the role of the primary unit.

- **Aid any injured third party.** If the suspect or primary unit strikes a pedestrian or another vehicle, be prepared to assist any injured victims.

You should also know your policy's guidelines on officers not directly involved in the pursuit. The most effective and safe way to pursue is with a primary unit and one backup. That is why many agencies allow only a supervisor to authorize bringing in more than two vehicles. But that does not mean that you should ignore the pursuit if you are not one of the participating units.

Guidelines for Officers Not Involved in the Pursuit

- **Pay attention to radio transmissions.** Keep track of the location, direction and speed of the pursuit. Think about what route to take if you are called upon to assist.

- **Do not get involved unless instructed to do so.** A large number of units flocking to the area will only cause confusion. You may be able to take up a position at a strategic location along the pursuit route. This might enable you to help stop traffic and minimize the risk to the general public. But do not take any action unless specifically authorized by the primary unit or a supervisor.

Pursuing in Allied Jurisdictions

It is possible that the suspect will lead you into the jurisdiction of another agency. Allied agencies frequently will not assume liability for a pursuit unless they have a clear understanding as to why it was initiated. If you were the primary unit when the pursuit began, you will probably be the primary unit when it ends. That being the case, you must know what is involved when pursuing outside your own jurisdiction.

Guidelines for Pursuing in Allied Jurisdictions

- **Follow your own policy.** Even when in another department's jurisdiction, you must continue to operate under your own agency's guidelines.

- **Be authorized.** In most cases, you need a specific directive from a supervisor or your policy to continue a pursuit that leaves your jurisdiction. Some areas even have laws that legally prohibit officers from pursuing into another jurisdiction.

- **Communicate with everyone involved.** Your supervisor and dispatch should know where you are at all times. In addition, most agencies will not participate in a pursuit unless they know the reasons for initiating it. If you cannot provide clear, concise reasons, you may have to terminate the pursuit.

- **Be prepared to assume a backup role.** If a unit from an allied agency takes over primary responsibility, request instructions on how you can assist. If more than one unit joins the pursuit, you may have to disengage completely.

Review Questions

1. What question should you repeatedly ask yourself during a pursuit?

2. What safety considerations should you follow when pursuing a suspect?

3. How can you help prevent a pursuit from becoming a personal challenge?

4. What are the limitations of emergency equipment in a pursuit?

5. According to your agency's policy, how many units can serve as backups in a pursuit situation?

6. If you are a backup unit, what are your responsibilities?

7. What is your agency's policy on pursuing a fleeing suspect into an allied jurisdiction?

Nineteen

Terminating a Pursuit

Objectives

After completing this chapter, you will be able to

- *List the factors that might lead to terminating without an apprehension*
- *Outline the steps for safely terminating without an apprehension*
- *Conduct a test of reasonableness for using force to terminate a pursuit*
- *Understand how to approach a suspect's vehicle*

You cannot continue a pursuit indefinitely. Lengthy pursuits pose too much of a threat to the general public. If the suspect will not stop, it is up to you to terminate the incident.

Termination without Apprehension

One option is to terminate the pursuit without apprehending the suspect. This is a very difficult decision to make. Most officers believe that terminating before a suspect is in custody goes against everything they stand for. In addition, the effects of emotions, peer pressure, frustration and social image can be enormous. However, you should never let personal issues get in the way of performing your duty. Your first obligation is to protect and serve the public. As stated in the previous chapter, **you must constantly perform the test of reasonableness** by asking yourself the following question:

Question to Ask while Pursuing

"Based on how the situation has changed, if this pursuit results in injury, death or property damage, would a reasonable person find that my actions were justified?"

As soon as a test of reasonableness shows that the risk of a continued pursuit outweighs the potential gain of an apprehension, your course of action is clear: **You must call off the pursuit**.

Remember that terminating without an apprehension is not the same thing as giving up. A successful pursuit does not always mean that you apprehend the suspect at that time. If you can identify the suspect and safely apprehend him later, then the pursuit is successful. After all, the objective is to get a dangerous criminal off the street without anyone being injured.

There are a number of factors that could lead you to terminate without making an apprehension. Several of them are listed below.

When to Terminate without Apprehension

- **The suspect has been identified and later apprehension poses no risk.** If you can apprehend the suspect later, then there is no need to continue a high-risk pursuit. This is assuming, of course, that the suspect is not an immediate threat to the public.

- **Your supervisor calls it off.** If a superior officer orders you to stop, then you must. To continue against orders could subject you to disciplinary proceedings within your own agency and direct liability in the courts.

- **Prevailing traffic makes the pursuit unsafe.** Any chase is dangerous, no matter when or where it takes place. However, if there is an increasing number of other motorists or pedestrians in the area, the risk that one of them will be injured will go up.

- **Your vehicle has a mechanical malfunction of any kind, especially emergency and communication equipment.** In most areas, you must use your emergency lights and siren to comply with state law. And if your radio does not work, you will not be able to maintain the communication necessary for a successful pursuit.

- **The suspect's vehicle is no longer in sight.** If you cannot see the vehicle, you should not pursue it. Instead, you might follow at a safe speed, without lights and siren, in the general direction that you last saw the vehicle. By coordinating your efforts with other units, you may be able to locate the suspect. This is another reason why communication is so important.

If you decide to terminate a pursuit without apprehending the suspect, there are several steps that you should follow.

Steps for Terminating without Apprehension

1. **Safely come to a complete stop and turn off your emergency warning devices.** As soon as traffic allows, pull off to the side of the road. Make it very clear that you are no longer in a pursuit mode. This is critical for the safety of the general public. You also want to let the suspect know that he is no longer being pursued. That might lead him to drive in a more responsible manner.

2. **Communicate your decision to terminate.** Contact the dispatch. When doing so, note the time, place and reason for your decision. You should also

indicate the speed and direction that the suspect vehicle is heading. That might hasten the suspect's apprehension.

3. **Get out of the vehicle for a few minutes.** Pursuing a fleeing suspect subjects you to high levels of physical and emotional stress. After terminating the pursuit, it is a good idea to exit your vehicle and take some deep breaths to help you calm down.

Terminating by Use of Force

In extreme cases, force can be used to terminate a pursuit. **Force is defined as any action on your part that willfully interferes with the suspect's path of travel or the operation of his vehicle.** Any intervention may cause the suspect to lose control of his vehicle. At the speeds normally associated with a pursuit, losing control of a vehicle frequently leads to great bodily harm or death. For that reason, forcefully terminating a pursuit could be considered a use of deadly force.

Using your emergency vehicle to physically terminate a pursuit could carry the same legal and moral implications as using your firearm. Force cannot be used simply to prevent an escape unless that force is controlled using a pursuit intervention technique that you have been trained to use. Since the application of force might be considered a violation of the suspect's right against unreasonable seizures, you must conduct a test of reasonableness before using force.

Question to Ask before Using Force

"If this suspect or another individual is injured or killed as the result of using force, would a reasonable person find that my actions are justified?"

To be justified, the situation must be life threatening. The suspect must have committed or be in the act of committing the type of offense that warrants the use of deadly force. In addition, you must believe that the continued movement of the suspect's vehicle would place others in imminent danger of serious physical injury or death. This threat must be such that it would still exist even if you called off the pursuit.

If you are going to apply force to terminate a pursuit, there will be a few steps you must follow. These are set by your state statutes and agency policy. The steps vary from state to state and agency to agency, but the following list will give you an idea of the sort of things that are usually required.

Guidelines for Using Force

- **Apply only those types of force that you are trained to use.** A lack of training is grounds for negligence. Just seeing someone else perform a maneuver is not enough. You must have had specific use-of-force training and be able to demonstrate how to use it.

- **Be authorized to use deadly force.** Your department's policy will be the guideline used to review the incident after it is over. For that reason, you must comply with this policy at all times. If you need authorization from a supervisor, get it before attempting any deadly force procedure. If you have the authority to make your own decision, apply the test of reasonableness.

- **Consider the area of deployment.** You cannot willfully endanger the public to terminate a pursuit, no matter how dangerous the suspect is. A reasonable person would not accept your shooting at a bank robber in a crowd of people. By the same token, a reasonable person would not accept your ramming another vehicle in a heavily congested area. Choose a location that minimizes the risk to the general public and everyone involved in the pursuit.

A common use of force to terminate a pursuit is a roadblock. Here are some examples.

Types of Roadblocks

- **Stationary roadblocks**—These are objects used to block the suspect's path of travel. They include electronic disablers, spike belts, and barricades. Most state statutes require that the obstacle be clearly visible and that the suspect has enough time to bring his vehicle to a safe, controlled stop after seeing it. In a further attempt to prevent a serious injury, most policies also require that a roadblock offers the suspect at least one avenue of escape.

- **Moving roadblocks**—Generally consists of using law enforcement vehicles to control or terminate the movement of a suspect's vehicle.

  —**Boxing in**—Several law enforcement vehicles are positioned so that the fleeing suspect has one of these vehicles in front, to the side and behind him. The cars then gradually slow down and force the suspect to the side of the road. It usually results in vehicle contact and poses a significant risk of injury to all participants.

  —**Forcing off the road**—This is driving along side the other vehicle and gradually moving into its path of travel. It often leads to contact and exposes you to significant danger. The suspect could easily run you off the road. A suspect with a gun could have a good line of fire.

  —**Precision Immobilization Technique (PIT)/ Tactical Vehicle Intervention (TVI)**—This is using the front quarter panel of your vehicle to intentionally push the rear quarter panel of the suspect's vehicle at an angle. The goal is to force the suspect's vehicle to spin into the opposite direction, allowing a back-up vehicle to block the suspect and make the apprehension.

—**Ramming**—This is intentionally making contact with the suspect. It often results in a loss of control for the suspect. It can also cause you to lose control of your vehicle. At the very least, your vehicle will sustain some damage as a result of this maneuver.

The Point of Termination

It is imperative that you **follow your agency's policy on high-risk or felony stops**. Every stop should be considered a high-risk situation. It does not matter if the suspect pulled over on his own or if you intervened with force; he is still dangerous. The incident is not over until the suspect is in custody.

When the suspect stops, place your vehicle so that you have a safe avenue of approach while giving optimum warning to the general public. For this reason, you should keep on your emergency lights. Your approach to the suspect's vehicle should be planned, deliberate and coordinated with other officers. Be prepared for the unexpected at all times.

Keep in mind that both the suspect and you have experienced a highly charged emotional event. Emotions such as excitement, fear, anger, anxiety and worry can have a crippling effect on decision-making. You must get control of your emotions because the number one concern is the safety of all parties involved. They include the general public, all officers and even the suspect who initiated the incident. For this reason, let officers who are not as emotionally caught up in the event handle the actual apprehension of the suspect whenever possible. This is a safeguard against the potential for mistreatment or an allegation of mistreatment.

In addition, the point of termination is the time to begin the documentation process. Special attention should be given to the facts that surround the incident. Constant mental awareness aids in developing complete, accurate reports.

Documentation Needs at the Point of Termination

- **Communicate with the dispatch.** Give the location and exact time of the stop. Provide vehicle and suspect descriptions. Also tell whether the suspect stopped on his own or you had to use force. Be precise as this will be part of the permanent record and will help you prepare after-action reports.

- **Secure the names of all parties involved.** This includes witnesses, citizens offering assistance and other officers and assisting agencies.

- **Account for all physical evidence and evidence preservation needs.** Evidence must be maintained not only at the point of termination, but also at the scene where the pursuit began and along the pursuit route.

Review Questions

1. According to your agency's policy, when should you terminate a pursuit without making an apprehension?

2. What factors might lead you to terminate a pursuit before apprehending a suspect?

3. What steps should you take if you terminate a pursuit without an apprehension?

4. Why is using force to terminate a pursuit often considered a use of deadly force?

5. What question should you ask yourself before using force to terminate a pursuit?

6. According to your policy, what types of force can be used to terminate a pursuit?

7. According to your policy, how should you approach the suspect vehicle after it has stopped?

Twenty

Pursuit Reporting and Analysis

Objectives

After completing this chapter, you will be able to

- *Use a systematic process for reporting*
- *Account for reporting errors in incident summaries*
- *Understand how to analyze your actions in a pursuit*

Since you will be held accountable for the actions you take during a pursuit, you have to be able to explain yourself. That is why reporting is so crucial. Good reporting starts with a system. This chapter shows you how to develop one.

Use Your Radio

The reporting process actually begins even before you start the pursuit. The moment you see a suspect commit the offense that led you to pursue, you have to account for all of your actions from that time until the incident is over. Your written report has to justify your reasons for initiating, continuing or terminating the chase. Since emotions always run high, remembering everything that happened when you sit down to write that report can be difficult. The job would be easier if you had some notes to refer to. Of course, you cannot stop and jot down information during a high-speed chase. But you can accomplish the same thing by using your radio.

Since everything transmitted to the dispatch and your supervisor is generally recorded, you can use your radio to take notes. This does not require any additional work since you should be communicating what is happening and what actions you are taking throughout a pursuit. After the incident is over, you can review the tape to make sure you address everything that occurred.

Tips for Using Your Radio for Reporting

- **Be complete.** Give a complete description of all events, from the time you first observe the suspect until the time you handcuff him and put him in the back seat of your vehicle. You must do more than just tell what is happening; you have to record the results of your various tests of reasonableness. That will help you justify your actions.

- **Be professional.** Do not make any comments that might reflect badly on the agency or you. Since everything that happens in a pursuit will generally be recorded, the tape of the incident will be one of the first things that a plaintiff's attorney will ask for in a lawsuit. If you come across as being overly aggressive, your credibility as a responsible law enforcement officer could be damaged. That will certainly impact your ability to defend a lawsuit.

Fill Out an Incident Report

After terminating a pursuit, you need to write down what happened. This should be done before you leave the scene or shortly thereafter, while the events are still fresh in your mind. At this stage of the reporting process, you do not need to be concerned about justifying your actions; you have already done that by using the radio. What you need to do is capture all of the facts, using an appropriate agency form.

Completing an Incident Report

- **You have to be systematic.** Just like the radio recording, an incident report may be discoverable evidence in a lawsuit. An incomplete report will call into question the validity of your reporting.

- **Note the times of all events.** Give accurate times for when the pursuit began and when it ended. If you terminate without an apprehension, be sure to indicate when you turned off your emergency equipment. This will be crucial information should a third-party accident occur after you indicated you were no longer in pursuit.

- **Identify all people involved in the pursuit.** Besides the suspect and yourself, identify the supervisor, assisting units from your agency, units from allied agencies, other occupants in the suspect's vehicle and any third parties that became involved. It is especially important to list those present at the scene of termination. You may need witnesses to verify facts should you be accused of inappropriate actions.

- **Be truthful.** False reports are usually found out. There are a number of ways to verify information. A witness can almost always be found. The dispatch tape may also yield conflicting information. You must be truthful in all aspects because one falsehood tends to discredit the entire report.

Writing a Summary

At some point you have to put together a written summary of what happened. While the incident report gives the facts, the summary shows how you weighed those facts in a reasonable manner and decided to take the actions that you took.

Things to Remember when Writing a Summary

- **Use your policy as the basis of your summary.** Show how you stayed within the limits of your agency's guidelines. If there was any deviation from the policy, be sure to indicate why it occurred. An example might be that several units formed a caravan behind the suspect and you. If your policy states that no more than two units can be directly involved, you have to explain the caravan. If it was due to vehicles from an allied agency joining the pursuit, you might be able to show that the deviation was beyond your control.

- **Include the test of reasonableness.** Remember, if a problem arises from the pursuit, you will be judged by juries and individuals with the untrained person's point of view. The question you asked yourself throughout the incident was "Would a reasonable person find that my actions were justified?" With that in mind, you should address such issues as
  —Why you initiated the pursuit
  —Why you maintained the pursuit for as long as you did
  —Why you terminated the pursuit at that particular time and in that particular manner

- **Correct any errors in the dispatch tape or incident report.** Reporting mistakes do happen, especially in the heat of the moment of a pursuit or immediately afterwards when emotions are still running high. You cannot alter the original tape and incident report, but you can use the summary to explain why the mistake was made. If all of the information does not correlate, a plaintiff's attorney could use that against you. As long as you catch and explain the error, however, your credibility will remain intact.

New information may surface over time. This information may be the result of follow-up investigations, records inquiries, collision reconstruction or evidence processing. As new information becomes available, it should be added to the incident summary by way of supplemental reports.

Post-Pursuit Review and Analysis

Every agency should mandate a review after each pursuit. This gives your supervisor and you the chance to evaluate the entire incident. Your supervisor can reinforce your positive actions as well as identify areas for improvement. When analyzing an incident, discuss everything that took place, from when you first observed the suspect to the point of termination. For each stage of the pursuit, consider the following questions:

Questions to Use in Analyzing a Pursuit

- Did all of your actions conform to the agency's policy?
- Were all of your decisions the correct ones to make?
- Were other options available for each action?
- If presented with the same situation again, what would you do differently?
- Did your agency's policy reflect the reality that you faced on the street?

It is essential that you identify any instances where you deviated from your agency's policy and take corrective action. Without correction, you will likely repeat that behavior the next time you are faced with a similar incident. In effect, this will negate the agency's policy and lead to a situation where the "real" policy of the agency is being developed on the street.

While a pursuit policy cannot be developed on the street, it should reflect street reality. If you find that your policy is inadequate, discuss the problem with your supervisor and administrators. Keep in mind, however, that an effective policy

159

must address the needs of a number of groups. These include the department, your supervisors, your fellow officers and the community in general. So instead of making demands, make recommendations. If you approach a problem in a professional manner, you can help solve it.

Review Questions

1. What are the components of your agency's pursuit reporting system?

2. What two steps should you follow when using your radio?

3. When filling out a pursuit incident report, what four things should you keep in mind?

4. What three things should you remember when making a written report of a pursuit?

5. What questions should you use to analyze a pursuit after it is over?

6. What are the proper procedures that you should follow to help correct a policy that does not address your needs?

Twenty-one

Lawsuits

Objectives

After completing this chapter, you will be able to

- *Identify the steps for preparing for a lawsuit*
- *Identify guidelines for testifying*
- *Understand how to react after a case is over*

No amount of policy development or training can prevent lawsuits. As long as there are injured parties who retain attorneys, cases will continue to be filed. Once you accept that you cannot prevent a lawsuit from happening, you can focus on what you can do to defend against one. In one sense, preparing for a lawsuit is "after the fact" risk management. This chapter helps you do that.

Initial Preparation

Preparation for the defense of a lawsuit occurs long before the first legal paper is ever filed. What steps you take to prepare depend upon the practices of your department. Principal among these is that each critical incident should be reviewed and analyzed, regardless of its outcome. This should occur even if no injuries or property damage occurred during the incident.

You should **take immediate steps after an incident to preserve information** that is needed for a review and that may be crucial to the defense of both your agency and you should a lawsuit ever be filed. This should include identifying attributes of the location where the incident occurred that might have an impact on the court case. You should not wait until you are faced with a lawsuit before gathering this information. Due to the length of statutes of limitations that may apply, there may be a gap of years between when an incident occurred and when a lawsuit is filed. Your best chance to build a defense is to start building one before you need it.

You might not like everything you uncover when you gather this information, but you still must make your best effort to capture and report all the facts. A plaintiff's attorney will likely discover anything that might damage your case. The only way your attorney can adequately defend you is if he or she knows everything. Never take a stonewall approach. That almost always backfires.

Besides protecting evidence, **you must also take care of yourself**. A lawsuit is very stressful. To participate effectively in your defense, you must know that your actions were appropriate under the circumstances. Just as important, you must also exhibit the confidence that those actions were appropriate. Do not hesitate to seek counseling after a serious incident. You will likely have to relive an incident during a lawsuit. If emotional wounds are left unattended, they could surface to cause serious damage to your defense.

Preparing for a Lawsuit

You should never view a lawsuit as an insult or a personal challenge. Being angry is normal, but you cannot let it consume you. Instead, trust that the judicial system will handle your case fairly. Channel your energies into developing the best possible defense. This starts by understanding the plaintiff's allegations. If you are unclear why the plaintiff has alleged a particular violation, ask your attorney to explain. The better you understand the charges, the better you will be able to defend against them.

Once opposing parties have been notified of a lawsuit, each side will begin a process generally known as **discovery**.

Discovery is governed by the Rules of Civil Procedure as defined by state or federal statutes. These rules identify what items of information you must disclose to an opposing party, when you must disclose them, and the consequences for not disclosing them. Many cases are settled or dismissed based upon what has been discovered by the opposing parties.

You should **meet with your attorney as early as possible** to review your case. Because so many lawsuits are settled before going to trial, it is crucial that you provide your counsel with accurate and thorough information. Plaintiff attorneys will pull out all stops to win a case. The last person you should hide the truth from is the person who will defend you.

Also, do not be surprised if you have to educate your defense counsel about the strategies and tactics of the incident. Most lawyers do not have the same operational knowledge that you do about something like conducting a pursuit. Work with your lawyer as you would a partner.

Issues to Discuss with Your Attorney

- **The facts of the incident**—You must know exactly what happened in the incident and be able to talk clearly about those facts.

- **The policy in question**—You must be able to explain the agency policies pertaining to the incident. You must also be able to discuss the agency's practices as they apply to that event.

- **The incident documentation**—Be prepared to furnish incident reports and documents that are complete and accurate. Also be prepared to explain and expand on those reports if questions are raised.

Your attorney and you should also **review the witness lists for both sides of the case**. You may be able to provide perspective on the information your attorney will get from each of your witnesses. Regarding the plaintiff's list, you should check to see that you recognize each name and know what each witness will testify to. You do not want any surprises in a lawsuit. If you don't know what a witness will say, further investigation is needed.

Another critical aspect of the discovery process is the **deposition**. At a deposition, attorneys from both sides have the opportunity to ask questions about specific issues pertaining to the case. You cannot lose your case at this point, but you will find out just how strong your defense is. Since the strength of your defense might lead to a settlement prior to trial, you must not take a deposition lightly.

During a deposition, opposing attorneys will be looking for weaknesses they can exploit at trial. They will pour over the transcript and videotape of your deposition in an effort to find "hot button" issues they can push. So the way in which you answer questions is just as important as the answers themselves.

Testifying is nerve-wracking, but there are some guidelines you can follow to be an effective witness for your side. They are listed below.

Guidelines for Testifying in a Deposition

- **Be truthful.** This is far and away the most important rule. You testify under oath when you give a deposition. If you perjure yourself, you will abandon much of what you stand for, and you could end up being criminally prosecuted.

- **Be prepared.** Most cases do not make it to trial, so your deposition may be your only opportunity to tell your side of the case. Your attorney will coach you in what to expect, but you should review the policy, facts and incident reports just prior to testifying.

- **Be professional.** Dress appropriately and always appear interested in the proceedings. Show respect for all parties involved. Never act arrogant, disgusted or bored. As stated earlier, you cannot lose your case in a deposition, but acting disrespectful can cause serious damage.

As a word of caution, never speculate during a deposition. Do not pretend to know something you don't. And do not offer an answer just because you think it is something that somebody wants to hear. If you don't know the answer to a question, then simply admit that.

The Trial

If a settlement cannot be reached, your case will go to trial, where a jury will make the final decision. Keep in mind that you will be under scrutiny at all times during a trial, not just when you testify. As during your deposition, always dress and act in a professional manner. Show respect for the court, and pay attention throughout the case. Jurors will view you as one who is responsible for making important decisions about their safety. Behave in such a manner that they can maintain trust in you and see you as one who values that trust.

When you do testify, your attorney will lead you through a series of questions known as **direct examination**. This is where you will present your side of the case. At the end of direct examination, the plaintiff's attorney will have an opportunity for **cross-examination**. This is where the opposing counsel will question you in an attempt to exploit perceived weaknesses in your case. The guidelines for testifying in a trial are the same as those for a deposition, with a couple of additional items to keep in mind.

Guidelines for Testifying in a Trial

- **Be truthful.** Again, this is far and away the most important rule. You have taken an oath to tell the truth. Nothing is worth committing perjury.

- **Be prepared.** You prepare for a trial like you do for a deposition. Review facts of the incident, the policy in question, and the incident documentation. It is also essential that you review the transcript of your deposition. That will give you an idea of the types of questions you will face.

- **Be professional.** As before, always show respect and never act arrogant, disgusted or bored.

- **Be consistent.** You will lose credibility if your courtroom testimony differs significantly from your deposition, where you also testified under oath. You can clarify a previous response or expand upon it to clear up a discrepancy, but your basic testimony must be the same.

- **Be clear.** Keep your answers short. Talk in a normal voice and use proper language. Don't use jargon. The jury will be comprised of average citizens, none of whom are law enforcement officers. Make sure they can understand your answers.

When testifying, listen to all questions and answer them to the best of your ability. If you do not understand a question, ask the attorney to repeat it or restate it in a way you do understand. Think about the question before responding. Your answer should be based on the facts, and it should seem fresh, not too rehearsed. If you do not know the answer to a question, do not pretend that you do. Pause before answering any question that you think may be improper. This gives your attorney a chance to object. Should an objection be raised, do not give an answer until directed to do so by the judge. And above all, control your emotions. By staying calm and courteous, the jurors will likely perceive you as being knowledgeable, thoughtful and confident.

After completing your testimony, think back on your strong points and weak points. Ask your attorney for an opinion and for advice on how to be a better witness. The idea is to start preparing for the next case. You will likely testify again at some point in your career. Analyzing your performance now will help make you a stronger voice for both the agency and yourself in the future.

When the Case Is Over

Many officers take lawsuits personally and want to fight no matter what. However, not all cases go to trial. An out-of-court settlement is not necessarily an admission of wrongdoing. A financial reality in today's world is that all agencies have to choose their battles carefully. Perhaps the odds of prevailing in a court were not favorable. Or maybe it was more cost effective to settle the case than participating in a long, drawn-out endeavor. The decision to settle is usually made by the defense counsel, in consultation with the agency and the agency's insurance carrier. Your input is important, however, and you should have the opportunity to give it.

If the case does go to trial, there is always the possibility that the jury will find against you. Should that happen, do not overreact. Some officers who have lost pursuit cases have decided that they will no longer conduct pursuits, regardless of the situation. This is a self-defeating attitude and does not help anyone. Instead, try to turn a negative into a positive. Experience growth from the incident and learn from it.

Regardless of the outcome, your agency should conduct an organized debriefing after each case. This is an important risk management step that closes the loop back to the "front end" process that we discussed in the first chapter of this book. The participants in this debriefing should include all line officers involved, the supervisors involved, the attorney, the risk manager and representatives from the administration.

The purpose of the debriefing is to reinforce the positive aspects of the incident and to identify areas where the policy was not followed or where the policy was inadequate. For areas where the policy was not followed, the agency must take steps to ensure that all officers will follow the directives in the future. If not corrected, officers often continue to act in the same manner. This can lead to a custom of usage issue, where the actual policy of the agency is developed on the street.

For areas where the policy is deficient, all parties should strive to increase the policy's effectiveness. You should take an active part in that process. By working to create change where change is needed, you will help strengthen your agency and increase the well-being of the community you have sworn to protect.

Review Questions

1. What steps should you take to prepare for a lawsuit?

2. What are the keys to testifying in a deposition or a trial?

3. How should you respond when a case is over?

Policy Worksheet

Up to this point, we have presented the basic components of emergency vehicle operations. We tried to include your agency's policy in some of the end-of-chapter questions, but we could only address a small portion of it at a time. Now we will concentrate on the policy itself.

What follows is a list of many elements that frequently make up a good pursuit policy. You should use your policy and standard agency practices to answer the questions below each element. By doing that, you will begin to see how all aspects of emergency vehicle operations fits together.

Mission Statement and Rationale

- Why was a policy established for emergency vehicle operations?
- When pursuing a suspect, what is your objective?

Statutory Reference

- What does your state statute require for the operation of an emergency vehicle? How are emergency operations and pursuits different from non-emergency operations?

Initiation Factors

- Which officers are eligible to participate in a pursuit?
- What types of violations could possibly justify initiating a pursuit?

- What vehicles may be used for a pursuit? Under what circumstances is a vehicle not authorized to be used in a pursuit?
- What factors must you consider when determining whether to begin a pursuit?

Responsibilities of Officer Pursuing Suspect

- What information must you communicate via radio?
- What are your basic responsibilities in a pursuit?
- What factors must you consider when determining whether to continue a pursuit?
- Under what circumstances should you relinquish primary responsibility of a pursuit?
- If a person is injured in the course of a pursuit, what steps must you take? Is there ever a circumstance where a pursuit can be continued after a third party has been injured?

Responsibilities of Supervisor

- What are the responsibilities of a supervisor in a pursuit situation?
- If no supervisor is available, who should assume the supervisor's responsibilities?

Responsibilities of Communications Personnel

- What are the responsibilities of communications personnel?

Responsibilities of a Backup Unit

- What are the responsibilities of a backup unit?
- What actions by a backup unit are NOT permissible?
- When should a backup unit assume primary responsibility for a pursuit?

Pursuit Tactics

- What is the maximum number of units that can take part in a pursuit?
- What tactics are permissible for use in a pursuit? Which tactics are considered to be high risk? Under what circumstances can you use these tactics? What sort of training is required for each tactic?
- What tactics are NOT permissible under any circumstance?
- What action should you take when approaching an intersection?
- What is considered an adequate following distance?

Termination Considerations

- Who makes the decision to terminate a pursuit? Of all the people who can make that decision, who has the final say?
- Under what circumstances must a pursuit be terminated immediately?

The Use of Force

- When can force be used to terminate a pursuit?
- What types of force are permissible? What types of force are NOT permissible?
- For each type of permissible force, how must it be implemented?
- What steps must you take before using any means of force?

Pursuits Involving Other Agencies or Jurisdictions

- If you are involved in a pursuit with another agency or in another jurisdiction, whose policy will govern your actions?

- What must you do if a suspect that you are pursuing enters another jurisdiction?
- Under what circumstances are you permitted to join a pursuit being conducted by officers from another agency?

Apprehension/Post-Pursuit Responsibility

- If the suspect is apprehended, who should make the arrest?
- Who has controlling responsibility at the scene of termination?
- How should the scene of termination be handled if the alleged violations for which you are pursuing a suspect occurred in multiple jurisdictions?

After-Action Reporting

- What reporting process must you follow after a pursuit?
- What is the time frame for completing and filing a report?
- Who receives a copy of the report after it is filed?

Pursuit Critique and Review

- What is the process by which a pursuit is reviewed and analyzed?
- What is the time frame for completing a review?

Training

- What training requirements must you meet before engaging in a pursuit?
- Are periodic in-service programs or re-certification required?

Discipline

- What disciplinary actions might result if you fail to follow your agency's pursuit policy? What other consequences might happen?

Other Pursuit Considerations

- Does the policy contain any words or terms whose meanings are unclear? If "yes," request clear definitions from your supervisor.

Glossary

Acceleration: The rate of change of velocity. It can be an increase or decrease. It is expressed as feet per second.

Accident: That occurrence in a sequence of events which usually produces unintended injury, death or property damage.

Actual damages: See **damages, compensatory, actual or special**.

Acuity: The capacity or either eye to recognize small space intervals in the discrimination of form.

Adhesion point: A point in a curvature where the maximum amount of stress is on the vehicle's tires.

Anti-Lock Braking System (ABS): A system that prevents the wheels of a vehicle from locking up. It works by having sensors that detect lock-ups and sending signals to a brake modulator that releases pressure to allow the wheels to turn again. The system then reapplies pressure to maintain maximum braking.

Apex: (1) the highest point of something; (2) the point at which two sides of an angle meet or cross.

Apex of a curve: The point of a turn or curve where the vehicle first begins to exit; the highest point of a curve.

Balanced hand position: A wide grip on the steering wheel. Some prefer a 9 o'clock and 3 o'clock position; others prefer a 10 o'clock and 2 o'clock position.

Banked pavement: One side of the roadway is elevated, banked or higher than the opposite side; normally occurs during a curve. Also referred to as "super elevation." An engineering design technique to increase the traction (friction) of the vehicle to the road during cornering. If on a left-hand curve, it is known as positive banking.

Brake fade: The loss of braking efficiency, normally due to heat build-up resulting from excessive use.

Braking distance: The distance through which brakes are applied to slow a vehicle; the shortest distance in which a particular vehicle can be stopped by braking from a specified speed on a particular surface; the distance from application of brakes to collision or stop.

Brake lock-up: The application of brakes to the point that the wheels can no longer rotate.

Braking, threshold: The brakes are pressed firmly to a point just before lock-up and held at that point and the wheels never lose their rolling friction.

Centrifugal force: The force of a body in motion which tends to keep it continuing the same direction rather than following a curved path. Understeering is an example.

Centripetal force: The force on a body in a curved motion that is directed toward the center axis of rotation. The force required to keep a moving mass in a circular path. A force which acts or impels an object toward a center of rotation. Oversteering is an example.

Cohesion: The mutual attraction by which the elements of a body are held together. The sticking power between two surfaces.

Compensatory damages: See **damages, compensatory, actual or special**.

Condition, varying or ongoing: Those factors which have an influence on choices of speed, lane position or communication needs. Examples include lane width, legal limitations, lane selection, traffic flow, traffic density, traffic controls, roadway design and conditions, visibility, environmental conditions, time of day, and weather.

Constitutional tort: See **tort, constitutional**.

Cornering skid: See **skid, cornering**.

Counterskid: A skid in the opposite direction of the original skid due to overreaction by the driver. Synonymous with secondary skid.

Countersteer: Turning the front wheels to counter the effects of a previous turning movement or of a skid in order to put the vehicle on its intended course of travel.

Cross-examination: The process of a lawsuit where opposing counsel asks you questions about your role in an incident.

Crowned pavement: A roadway on which the center portion is higher than either of its sides.

Custom of usage: A legal concept where polices are developed based on how officers respond to a certain type of incident. Generally, these policies are not specific and allow a broad interpretation of acceptable procedures.

Damages, compensatory, actual or special: Money award in a lawsuit that compensates for the injury only.

Damages, punitive: Money awarded in a lawsuit over and above the compensatory levels. It serves as punishment for having caused the injury.

Deceleration: The rate of change of velocity when slowing down only.

Defendant: The person or entity in a lawsuit who is accused of causing the injury claimed in the lawsuit.

Defensive driving: Operating a vehicle in such a manner as to be able to avoid involvement in a preventable accident, no matter what the road and weather conditions. Synonymous with precision driving.

Deposition: Part of the discovery process of a lawsuit where attorneys for both sides ask a person questions about specific issues pertaining to the case.

Direct examination: The process of a lawsuit where your attorney asks you questions about your role in an incident.

Discovery: The initial process of a lawsuit whereby opposing parties are afforded access to certain types of information.

Drag factor: A number which has been assigned to scientifically describe the slipperiness of a surface. The higher the drag factor, the greater the resistance. Synonymous with friction coefficient.

Driving, emergency: A response to a situation that is life threatening or that involves an extreme property loss; justifies that legal use of an emergency warning device.

Driving, non-emergency: All operations of a vehicle in other than an emergency or pursuit mode, as defined herein.

Driving, precision: The operation of a vehicle in such a manner as to avoid involvement in a collision, no matter what the road and weather conditions or the actions of other drivers. Synonymous with defensive driving.

Driving, pursuit: The act or instance of chasing or pursuing a fleeing vehicle in an attempt to overtake and apprehend the driver.

Duty: An obligation of an agency to provide a service or protection.

Emergency: A situation that justifies the use of lights and siren. The precise definition varies from state to state. Some states have defined it as "a life or death situation;" others have listed an "assault" as being an emergency.

Emergency signal devices: A siren, flashing or revolving lights that meet the requirements of a state statutes. Synonymous with emergency warning devices.

Energy, kinetic: Energy associated with motion; the energy possessed by a body in motion. Kinetic energy = 1/2 mass x velocity squared. A force exerted by one solid surface on another when the two surfaces are sliding past each other. Distinguished from momentum.

Energy, potential: The energy a body possesses by virtue of its position, e.g., a vehicle parked on a hill. The energy stored in a spring as it is stretched or compressed.

Evasive action: Any action taken by a driver to avoid a hazardous situation or collision. Can be steering, braking or accelerating. Sometimes referred to as a tactic.

EVOC: An acronym for Emergency Vehicle Operation Course. A course involving the control of an emergency vehicle using emergency equipment.

Feet per second: An alternative miles per hour as a means of expressing speed. It is determined by multiplying m.p.h. by 1.47.

Force: That which changes the state of rest or motion of matter, measured by the rate of change of momentum. Mass times acceleration.

Force, gravitational: A constant force; gravity creates weight.

Force, inertia: The tendency of a body to resist acceleration; the tendency of a body at rest to remain at rest or a body in motion to stay in motion in a straight line unless disturbed by an external force.

Force, momentum: The product of a body's mass times velocity. An amount of motion; it is the property of a moving body which determines the length of time required to bring it to a rest. Distinguished from kinetic energy.

Friction: (1) The rubbing of one object or surface against another. (2) Resistance to any force trying to produce motion; constantly present and always working opposite the direction in which an object is moving.

Friction coefficient: The measurement of cohesion between two surfaces. Synonymous with drag factor.

Friction, rolling: A force exerted by one solid surface on another when the two surfaces are sliding past each other. A prerequisite to steering, e.g., the front wheels must be rolling in order to steer the vehicle.

Friction, static: A force exerted by one solid surface on another then they are at rest; the holding force between two surfaces at rest.

Front-end swing: The movement of the front end in the opposite direction of the steering input when backing up.

"Good faith" immunity: See **immunity, "good faith" or qualified**.

Handling: A vehicle's ability to quickly and accurately respond to a driver's command with no or minimal negative reaction, and the ability to compensate for sudden irregularities in road or wind conditions. Distinguished from ride.

Hydroplaning: To skim along on the surface of water. Occurs when a tire rides upon water rather than the roadway.

Immunity, "good faith" or qualified: A legal concept that protects a person from being held liable for behavior that does not violate "clearly established law."

Impact force: The force measured when one object collides with another. It includes the speed of the objects, the weight of the objects and the distance traveled between impact and the final resting place.

Impending skid: See **skid, impending**.

Inertia: See **force, inertia**.

Intentional tort: See **tort, intentional**.

Interactive triangle: The interplay of three components in any response or pursuit: the driver, the vehicle itself, and the environment where the incident takes place.

Invincibility Syndrome: A false sense of security stemming from the belief that the general public will properly respond to your emergency warning devices.

Kinetic energy: See **energy, kinetic**.

Known Risk: A risks that an officer should be aware of and can anticipate.

Longitudinal weight transfer: See **weight transfer, longitudinal**.

Lateral weight transfer: See **weight transfer, lateral**.

Liability, direct: The liability that is imposed upon a person for causing injury to another through a negligent or willful misconduct.

Liability, municipal: The liability that is imposed upon any agency of government below the state level for causing injury to a person or property through negligence.

Liability, vicarious or indirect: The liability which is imposed on one who is without personal fault or complicity because of the relationship that person bears towards the person who actually performed the wrongful act or omission.

Marked vehicle: See **vehicle, marked**.

Mental conditioning: The preparation of the driver to deal with the psychological, physiological and environmental conditions that may be encountered while operating a motor vehicle.

Momentum: See **force, momentum**.

Mechanics: A branch of the science of physics which deals with what happens when forces act on material objects.

Municipal liability: See **liability, municipal**.

Negligence: For civil litigation in some states, it is the failure of a law enforcement officer to conform his or her conduct to the standard which a reasonable law enforcement officer would have conformed under the same or similar circumstances. In other states, an officer is held to a standard of the "reasonable man."

Negligence per se: A legal concept where the violation of a statute in and of itself is regarded as negligence, regardless of the circumstances surrounding the event.

Newton's first law of motion: Every body continues in its state of rest or of uniform motion in a straight line unless acted upon by another force.

Newton's second law of motion: A change of motion is proportional to force applied and takes place in the direction of the line of action of the force.

Newton's third law of motion: To every action, there is always an equal and opposite reaction.

Oversteer: The characteristic of a vehicle to tighten its turning radius as the rear end slips toward the outside curve.

Patrol driving: See **driving, non-emergency**.

Perception: (1) Awareness of objects and other data through the medium of the senses; (2) having insight or intuition, as an abstract quality.

PIT/TVI: See **Precision Immobilization Technique/Tactical Vehicle Intervention**.

Plaintiff: The person who initiates a civil lawsuit.

Police package: A manufacturer's modification of a standard passenger vehicle to meet the demands placed on a police patrol vehicle. It usually involves modification of the braking, suspension and electrical systems.

Potential energy: See **energy, potential**.

Power skid: See **skid, power**.

Precision driving: See **driving, precision**.

Precision Immobilization Technique/Tactical Vehicle Intervention (PIT/TVI): An application of force technique whereby an officer intentionally uses his or her emergency vehicle to push a suspect vehicle at an angle from the rear, causing the suspect vehicle to spin out of control so that apprehension can be effected.

Punitive damages: See **damages, punitive**.

Pursuit: An event involving a peace officer attempting to apprehend a person in a motor vehicle while that person is trying to avoid capture by willfully failing to yield to the officer's signal to stop.

Qualified immunity: See **immunity, "good faith" or qualified**.

Reaction time: The total length of time it takes for the brain to receive the information from the senses (eyes, ears, nose), make a decision, transmit the decision to the appropriate muscles and for the muscles to respond.

Rear end cheat: While driving forward during a turn, the rear tires will track along a path different than that of the front tires. They may track inside, outside or along the same line, depending on the speed, tires and load distribution.

Responded superior: Latin for "let the master answer." The legal theory that the employer is liable for the wrongful acts of the employee where the employee is acting within the scope of employment. This theory is applicable only in state tort claims. It is not applicable in constitutional tort claims.

Ride: The result of a vehicle's absorption of the irregularities of the road. This is accomplished through the design of tires and suspension system (springs, shock absorbers). Distinguish from handling.

Risk: A hazard to which you are exposed when taking a certain action.

Risk management: A concept whose objective is to identify things that may cause injury or harm and then take steps in advance to prevent them from happening.

Rolling friction: See **friction, rolling**.

Semi-marked vehicle: See **vehicle, semi-marked**.

Siren: A device used to generate and transmit the easily recognized siren sound whose frequency varies with time, used as a warning signal by police vehicles, fire vehicles and ambulances. There are three types of sirens: electro-mechanical, electronic and mechanical.

Skid: The loss of traction to one or more wheels.

Skid, braking: The loss of traction when one or more wheels are locked by excessive braking pressure.

Skid, cornering: The of traction in negotiating a curve or a turn at a speed faster than can be sustained by the tire-road cornering traction limits.

Skid, impending: A preliminary skid caused by maximum pedal pressure short of locking the brakes. Sometimes improperly used as a synonym for threshold braking.

Skid, power: The loss of traction when excessive power is applied, causing the drive wheels to spin and no longer provide cornering traction.

Skid pan or pad: An area designed to practice skid control.

Space cushion: The open area surrounding a vehicle while it is in motion. An "escape route" to the front, rear and sides.

Space management: The selection of the best speed control, path of travel or communication technique to maximize control of the space surrounding the vehicle.

Spatial: Relating to or involving space.

Special damages: See **damages, compensatory, actual or special**.

Speed, high: A speed that would constitute reckless driving, given the posted or prima facie speed.

Speed, moderate: 50% to 75% of the maximum speed at which a vehicle may be safely operated, considering the nature, condition and type of roadway, volume and direction of the flow of traffic, presence of intersections, visibility and weather conditions.

Strategy: An overall plan to increase the probability of success and to minimize the probability of failure. Distinguished from tactic.

Supervisor: An individual having responsibility for the control or training of others.

Tactic: The actions of an individual or small group for achieving a limited goal or objective. Distinguished from strategy.

Time spatial judgment, rate of closure: Ability to judge the proper rate of deceleration to avoid a hazard.

Tire footprint: The contract area of a tire tread with the roadway.

Tort: A private or civil wrong against a person or property for which a court may award money damages.

Tort, constitutional: A private or civil wrong against a person or property resulting from the violation of a right guaranteed by the United States Constitution.

Tort, intentional: A wrongful act committed by a person who knows that the law requires that the act not be committed.

Track: The distance on the ground between the center of the tire tread on one side of the vehicle to the center of the parallel tire tread on the opposite side.

Tunnel vision: A narrow arc of vision. The focus of attention on a particular object or area to the exclusion of adjacent areas of activity.

Universe of Risks: The complete set of risks that you face while performing a given task.

Under steer: The tendency of a vehicle to continue in a straight line and resist turning from a direct course of travel. The result is a tendency to swerve toward the outside of a curve. Motor vehicles with more weight on front wheels than on rear or with too little pressure in front tires is likely to under steer at high speed.

Unknown Risk: A risk that is unpredictable, and as such, one that you have no control over.

Vehicle control: Developing an understanding of the principles and developing the proficiency pertaining to the successful operation of vehicles under all driving conditions.

Vehicle dynamics: Any force, action or law of physics that affects the path of a vehicle in motion.

Vehicle, marked: A police patrol vehicle equipped with a permanent emergency roof light, siren and police agency vehicle identification decals. It may or may not be painted with standard colors.

Vehicle, semi-marked: A police patrol vehicle equipped with a siren and permanent emergency lights in the grill area or mounted in the front or rear window area.

Vehicle, unmarked: A standard vehicle with no indicators that it is a law enforcement vehicle. It may or may not be equipped with portable or concealed emergency lights and siren.

Velocity: The time rate of motion in a fixed direction; the rate of change of position relative to time; speed of motion in a particular direction.

Vision, peripheral: A wide arc of vision that allows a person to see objects to the right and left of center.

Visual horizon: The point at which a driver's eyes are focused on the roadway.

Wheelbase: The distance from the center of the front wheel to the center of the rear wheels.

Weight transfer: The transfer of weight to the front, rear or either side caused by acceleration, deceleration or turning.

Weight transfer, lateral: The transfer of weight to the opposite side of the vehicle due to a turn.

Weight transfer, longitudinal: Transfer of weight to the rear axle due to acceleration or to the front axle due to deceleration.

Index

Occupant protection devices, 42-43
Overconfidence, 48

Passing, 76-77
Passive safety components, 4-45
Paying damages, 8
Peer pressure, 93-94
Plaintiff, 8
Policy, 20, 124-126, 161-165
Post-pursuit analysis, 159
Preoccupation, 49-50
Punitive damages, 10
Pursuit procedures, 135-138

Qualified immunity, 24

Radio, 68-69, 103-104, 137-138, 155
Reckless behavior, 9
Reckless negligence, 9
Respondeat superior, 12
Risk management, 27-33, 167
Road condition, 81-83
Roadblocks, 150-151
Route selection, 109-111

S.I.P.D.E., 40-41
Safety belt, 42-43
Self-righteousness, 49
Simple negligence, 8-9
Skid,78-79
Smith system, 39-40
Space management, 114-115
Special damages, 10
Speed, 59-60, 91-93, 98-99
Speed progression, 139
State statute, 18-19
Steering, 100

Steering, 62-63
Stimulants, 53
Stress, 52
Substance abuse, 52-54
Sudden mechanical failure, 58

Test of reasonableness, 127-128, 134-135, 145-146
Testifying, 164-166
Tort, 7
Trial, 164-166
Turns, 73-75

"U" turns, 74
"Universe of Risks", 28
Use of force, 148-151

Vehicle inspection, 56-57
Vicarious liability, 11-13

Weather conditions, 85-87
Weight transfers, 98
Willful or wanton negligence, 9

Zone control system, 41-42

Check out these other books available from K&M Publishers, the new leader in law enforcement publishing!

Critical Incident Management
An On-Scene Guide for Law Enforcement Supervisors

Vincent F. Faggiano
Thomas T. Gillespie

Defensible Policies
Developing and Implementing Valid
Policies for Problem-Oriented Policing
Second Edition

Raymond W. Beach, Jr.
James S. O'Leary

Disaster Dictionary
A Guide to Terms, Acronyms, Concepts and Certifications
Used for Emergency Planning and Operations

Daniel J. Biby

For information on these and other upcoming titles, contact

K&M Publishers, Inc.
P.O. Box 701083
Tulsa, OK 74170

800-831-4210 / www.kmpub.com